Home
Educating
with CONFIDENCE

How Ordinary Parents CAN
Produce Extraordinary Children

Rick & Marilyn Boyer

HOME EDUCATING WITH CONFIDENCE

©1996 by Rick and Marilyn Boyer

Cover design by Mark Dinsmore

Book design by Brian Michael Taylor, 2Cor3:3

ISBN 0-9645396-3-2

Published by Homeschool Press
229 S. Bridge Street
PO Box 254
Elkton MD 21922-0254

Send requests for information to the above adress.

Printed in the United States of America

*Dedicated to
the Moms and Dads
of the home-education movement
whose homes are the seedbeds
of the coming revival.*

❦

*Today they rock the cradle;
tomorrow their children
will rock the world.*

*And those from among you
will rebuild the ancient ruins;
You will raise up
the age-old foundations;
And you will be called
the repairer of the breach,
The restorer of the streets
in which to dwell.*

—ISAIAH **58:12** NASB

CONTENTS

Part I Thinking It Over

Part II Hitting The Books

Part III Other Things

Afterword

Part 1

Thinking It Over

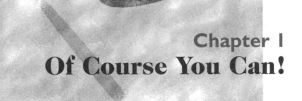

Chapter 1
Of Course You Can!

THE **PRIMARY PURPOSE** of this book is to encourage you. Whether you are home educating now or considering it for the future, you won't have to go far to find someone who will be happy to tell you you're crazy and doomed to failure. As a matter of fact, I happen to think they're crazy. So, in the interest of fairness and balance, I have taken it upon myself to provide equal time. My suggestion is that the next time someone takes it upon himself to lecture you on the danger of making babbling, glassy-eyed idiots out of your children, glance occasionally at your watch during his harangue. Then politely end the conversation and as soon as possible open this book and begin to read. If your friend (or mother, or whoever) lectured you for, say, ten minutes, then read for the same amount of time. Alter having endured ten minutes of criticism you deserve ten minutes' worth of support.

But encouragement is not our only purpose here. As I tell my audience in the first session of the Learning Parent Home Education Seminar, our purpose is fourfold. First, as I said, we do want to encourage you that you are perfectly capable of teaching your children and teaching them well. Second, we want to give you some Biblical guidelines and foundation for home education. Third, we want to give you some practical, hands-on how-to's for the job at hand. And fourth, we want you to have a good time. That's all, just enjoy yourself. There's enough stress in parenthood, especially outside the mainstream, to make it necessary to just relax and chuckle occasionally.

If you're considering home education but nervous about taking the plunge, or if you're teaching at home now but not confident that you're making the grade,

4

Chapter I **Of Course You Can!**

relax and think things over for a while. You probably know families who have fewer advantages than you have but are home educating and loving it. If not, let me introduce you to one.

Meet the Boyers. My wife Marilyn and I have been teaching our children at home since kindergarten. If we can do it, you can too. You don't have a college education? Neither do we. You aren't a certified teacher? Neither are we. You have several children to deal with? We have twelve. You're under financial pressure? When our ninth child was born I was still making under twenty-five thousand dollars a year. You're afraid a lot of people will think you're strange? Relax. A lot of people are sure we're strange.

I say all this so you won't think you're being lectured by a guy who, along with his wife, has it all together and goes through every day without a ruffled hair. Au contraire. And what's more, it ain't so. We have our share of pressures and failures, and in fact we do approach mental meltdown occasionally. But we've been home educating for fourteen years under less-than-ideal circumstances and we absolutely wouldn't consider any other method of educating our children.

Don't get me wrong. Home education isn't a cure-all for every educational or behavioral problem your children have ever had. I'm not among those who believe that if you just turn your children loose to spend their time as they see fit and give them good books they will naturally give themselves a fine education with no effort on their parents' part. There are some cautions and I wouldn't encourage you to go full-speed ahead without giving them full consideration. As a matter of fact, I long ago stopped encouraging people to home educate without regard to their circumstances. I came to realize that we are in a movement that still has a distance to go in securing legal and social acceptance for our lifestyle and that those who jumped in to test the water without counting the cost were not the best prospects for success. We need to produce children who will be good testimonials for home education in order to not give the whole movement a black eye. We are, after all, still in the process of educating the public to the fact that we're here to stay and we're really not crazy. But having said that, I'll leave the rest of the caveat for later in the book. My purpose here is to assure you that you can handle it.

Don't think because you haven't been to college and don't have teaching experience that home education won't work for you. So much of what is taught to students in teachers' colleges is based on the falsehoods of psychology, sociology, and statism that you're better off as you are. After all, what is so difficult about teaching? Most of what we learn in life we learn from people who aren't paid teachers. For instance, some girls take home economics in high school and learn to cook, sew, care for babies, etc. But by the time they're married and have a child a year or two old, they know far more about those things than they learned or could have learned in school. Furthermore, what they learn after marriage (and often in their own homes before marriage) is impressed much more solidly in their minds and comes without the assistance of a teaching professional.

The same principle applies to many different types of information. If you know something about history or science or mathematics, don't you think you could teach

Chapter 1 **Of Course You Can!**

that information to just about anyone who is interested? John Gatto has pointed out that professional interest is best served by making that which is easy to do seem difficult. In other words, professional educators have a stake in conditioning the public to believe that school people are a sort of aristocracy endued with ability and high-tech training far beyond the reach of those lower on the food chain. But if you'll stop and think about it a minute, it should be obvious that that doesn't make sense. Anyone who has been long in the workforce has acquired a tremendous amount of his job knowledge from bosses and co-workers, and has taught some of that to others. Usually, none of the parties involved has spent any time in a teachers' college. Yet the mills of industry and commerce grind on daily with few major glitches other than the low quality of the employee material being turned out by the professionals in the schools. Still it is these professionals who attack home educators as *unqualified*. Small wonder. If the public continues to wake up to the incompetence of the public school system, a revolution of private education looms on the horizon and a lot of *educrats* will be out of work.

If professional training were in fact the key to good learning, the public schools would be mass producing excellence. Teachers not only have to complete a college degree (usually) and certification, but they also are required to continually "upgrade" their education with supplemental courses from time to time in order to remain certified. The assumption that this ensures good education has been repeatedly used as leverage by school groups opposed to home education in their quest to get state governments to require certification of parents. But the theory hasn't stood up in court when parents have been challenged on their teaching. Plenty of studies have demonstrated that certification of teachers absolutely does not correspond with good teaching.

The public school system is now spending over $6,000 per year on each student enrolled. That's about three times what it costs to send a child to one of the several private Christian schools in the area in which we live. And what are the taxpayers getting for their money? The United States ranks at or near the bottom of the list when compared with fifteen or twenty industrialized countries in critical academic subjects. A friend of mine who is a supervisor for a local fast food restaurant says he is constantly plagued with incompetence on the part of the high school students they employ. Many, he says, are unable to make correct change or read well enough to tell the difference between a Whopper box and a Whaler box.

Of course the school system cries about insufficient funding and blames everybody from families to society at large for the problems, but their camouflage is wearing thin. The taxpayers are losing patience, as they should have long ago, with a system that eats up an ever-increasing amount of money and spits out graduates who, in some cases, can't even read their diplomas. If you're hesitating about home education because you're not part of that educational cadre, relax. That fact may be your best qualification.

Overall, statistics are on your side. Home education as a national trend is old enough now that there is a broad base of research showing that it works for ordinary moms and dads. Studies show home-educated children scoring consistently higher, and in some surveys

Chapter I **Of Course You Can!**

as much as thirty percent higher than their schooled counterparts.

Some parents struggle with the preconception that parents aren't teachers as teachers aren't parents. The general acceptance of that idea isn't surprising when you consider that most of us have spent twelve or more years of our lives in an environment that separates where we learn from where we live. A veteran school teacher once told me that she (despite her master's degree in education) couldn't teach her own children. She explained that they wouldn't listen to her, though they would listen to another teacher. This interesting phenomenon is understandable when one considers that most children are sent away from home and parents each day to a place whose sole purpose is supposed to be learning. That specialized institution is staffed by specially trained professionals whom the children know in no other role than as teachers. Most of the things that happen at school don't happen at home and most of the things that happen at home don't happen at school. Small wonder then that many children, after several years of this indoctrination, identify teachers as the only adults whose opinions count in matters of academics. The singular niche of teachers in the mind of the child was illustrated hilariously in a cartoon I saw recently: A mom comes home from grocery shopping one summer day and remarks to her little boy that she had seen his teacher in the store. He seems surprised to hear of an institutional icon frequenting the familiar neighborhood market. "Why, sure," his mother explains. "Teachers have to buy groceries, too. What'd you expect?" "I dunno," says the little boy contemplatively. "I guess I just always assumed teachers slept in a coffin all summer."

I don't know where all teachers sleep, but if you have children at least one teacher sleeps in your bed. It doesn't take a profound thinker to see that parents teach constantly. While many of the important lessons of early life appear to be mostly self-taught (and don't forget that when the time comes to open the textbooks), parents are undeniably key players in that learning. Parents help little children learn to walk, talk, dress themselves, feed themselves, get along with others, do household chores, manage the garden, care for pets, and perform a long list of other important functions—some of which are included in the subject matter of college courses. Yet when children reach the age of learning to read, write and do arithmetic, when the doors begin to open on a huge and fascinating world, along comes the social pressure, and in some cases the law, telling parents that it's time to surrender the pleasure of watching their little one learn and turn him over to the ever-benevolent state. He needs professional instruction now, you know. You mustn't think that the fact that you've been his teacher for five or six years means you're capable of teaching him m the future. Why, this year he'll be facing such monumental challenges as the alphabet!

When Marilyn and I decided fourteen years ago to teach our eldest son at home, we were thinking only in terms of kindergarten. We then had four little boys, and the commute to the Christian preschool attended by the two older ones was hard on Mom and the two babies. I was a little shocked when my wife suggested that she teach Rickey at home the following year because at that time I had never heard of home education. But because Marilyn was a sharp girl and had done some student teaching, I foresaw no problem. It was, after all, just for kindergarten.

Chapter 1 Of Course You Can!

We were only a few weeks into the first year of home education when we decided it was working so well we'd continue it another year. Before first grade ended, we saw no need to send the children to school at all.

We had discovered what thousands of other couples have learned before and since. Home education, in a healthy and well-ordered home, is simple and natural. I hesitate to use the word easy, as nothing about raising children strikes me as easy. But teaching our own children, in our own way, with our own choice of materials, and at their own natural pace bears little resemblance to the job that faces a teacher in a classroom of thirty students. We have all the advantages of the small student-teacher ratio, much better discipline than in most classrooms, far less busywork, a wide choice of good text materials and above all, a deep bond of love with our children.

I don't want to give the prospective home educator an unbalanced picture, but my experience has been that most people seem to think that home education is a difficult and laborious process that strains to the utmost a parent's time, ability, and patience. Marilyn and I have not found that to be the case at all. And while we don't want you to stroll into the matter with a Pollyanna attitude and a sappy grin, we feel compelled to present the other side of the picture. That side says, in a nutshell, that home education comes naturally to the extent that you can divest your thinking of the schoolish notions you've absorbed from your upbringing. If you try to make your home into a school and do all the things schools do, you'll make a lot of hassle for yourself and the results won't be what they should. But if you approach teaching academics to your children in the same natural, sensible way in which you taught them the other skills of life, you'll find that home education is productive, interesting, and fulfilling for parents and children.

You probably know home educators who act as if teaching their children is a great burden. In those cases, usually the problem isn't home education per se, but either a source of pressure that is not directly related to education or a problem with the way the educating is being done. For instance, a lot of young families are under financial pressure and are constantly distracted by the emotional stress. This problem occurs in families whether they are home educating or not, but when home education is a part of the picture the learning aspect often suffers. Still, it's important to understand that the root problem is not that the children are educated at home. It's external to the teaching process. When the problem is actually in the teaching-learning relation itself, it's usually the result of doing things in an unwise way or a simple blind spot on the part of the parent that can be corrected without major surgery.

Don't let the obstacles you face (or anticipate facing in the future) discourage you from teaching your children. Help is available from quite a variety of sources. Ten years ago many parents had to stand alone when they ran into snags but the picture is vastly different today. There are state and local support associations, seminars, conventions and a wide variety of new businesses springing up to supply the needs of home educators. Some of them want to give you even more help than you need, but you'll learn to weed out the fluff and ferret out the nuggets. You may very well not feel a need for association with any of these groups and if not, don't wonder if that makes you an oddball. Marilyn and I are constantly trying to convince

Chapter 1 Of Course You Can!

parents that home education is generally simple and that most of them really don't need a lot of help.

There was a time when the parent's options for teaching materials seemed limited. No more. The home education market is now so huge that publishers are scrambling to get a piece of the action. Characteristic of the trend is one publisher with whom we do considerable business, who at one time refused to sell to home educators because they didn't believe in the home-learning concept. Within a few years our ranks had swollen to make us a multi-million dollar market and this publisher began to see the light. Today they make big money in home-education sales and the concept doesn't look quite so bizarre after all. They and scores of other vendors now make table reservations months and years in advance to jam display booths at conventions and book fairs, offering a bewildering array of programs and products that are far more than you could ever use. Many of them advertise in various home-education magazines, several of which now exist. The problem now is not finding enough stuff to use, but sorting out what's useful and what's not.

Legal matters are not the problem they once were, either. As one who navigated the legal swamp in our state prior to the advent of legislation favorable to home teaching, I'm very thankful for the improvement. Marilyn and I were taken to court over the issue and it wasn't fun. That was twelve years ago. Now there are legal-protection associations and non-profit legal-aid groups for the defense of home educators. (Whew.) We'll list some of those for you later in the book.

If you're worried that educating your children will be exhausting and time-consuming, relax. My wife has eight children in the classroom and a crawler underfoot each day. Yet she rarely spends more than two hours per day in structured teaching. Why? Because individualized instruction is so much more effective than school. Remember in fourth grade when you were out for a week with the chicken pox? You missed thirty or thirty-five hours in the classroom. But it didn't take anywhere near that many hours to catch up. Chances are your parents brought your books from school (thanks a lot, Mom) and you spent an hour or two per day toward the end of your sick week working on assignments, and then finished catching up the first week back at school. That's the difference between individual study and learning in a group of thirty, where busywork and mob control are involved.

To end this chapter I'd like to reiterate my belief that any healthy Christian family is capable of educating its children at home. Most people make it harder than it is by doing things the way they've seen them done in schools instead of setting their own family goals and pursuing them according to the dictates of their own good sense. If you are considering starting to teach your children at home and you're being told you aren't qualified, just ask around until you find some families who are doing it well and happily. They'll tell you how they do it and you'll see how you can do it too. If you are a home educator and growing weary in well doing, don't give up and put your children back in the institution. Get some wise counsel (meaning from successful parents, not some shrink), keep analyzing, and correct problems when you find them. In either case, read on and we'll try to give you some useful information and encouragement.

Chapter 1 **Of Course You Can!**

> *We have all the advantages of the small student-teacher ratio, much better discipline than in most classrooms, far less busywork, a wide choice of good text materials and above all, a deep bond of love with our children.*
>
> —RICK BOYER

Chapter 2
Doing It God's Way

T HE PREVAILING PROBLEM in Christian home education is one of models. It's a fact of human nature that we tend to do things as we have seen them done. That's why we often get into trouble and yet can't see where we've done anything wrong. Finances are a good example. The Bible tells us to do some things concerning money that the rest of the world would consider counterproductive, such as tithing and avoiding debt. What? Give away ten percent of your money? That's your savings! And live without borrowing? You have to have capital. It takes money to make money. Besides, there are other things you'll want before you have the cash available. Why not let your family be enjoying them while you're paying for them? These ideas sound quite logical to most people, but God knows there is a better way.

The same applies in any number of areas. The world says don't get mad, get even. Scripture says turn the other cheek. The world says to look out for Number One, Scripture says to put others before self. The world says men and women are in competition with each other, Scripture says woman was given as a helper because it is not good that man should be alone.

So it is with the training of children. God has given us a plan in Scripture if we'll search it out and apply it. But most of us haven't been taught to approach life's responsibilities that way, so we do it as we've always seen it done. When it comes time to hit the books, we ship our little ones off to school.

Home educators have taken one important step back toward the Scripture model by rejecting institutional school. But doing that is only scratching the surface. Most of us, even though we have rejected school, are still doing

Chapter 2 Doing It God's Way

to our children much of what is done in schools. The next step, and the step that most home educators never take, is to go back to the Bible and identify the elements of God's plan for child-rearing.

There is considerable pressure on the parent not to do this. In our society, at least in our time, mass schooling has carved a niche for itself in the national psyche. It has come to be regarded as a great American institution, a state-of-the-art system that has sprouted, grown, and adapted with the changing needs of the population. That's hogwash. The public school system is a mammoth failure. But its image as the industry standard for education is fostered by the billions of dollars we spend on it, the professional esteem bestowed upon its practitioners, and the massive structure we've built to maintain it. It's really no wonder that individual humble parents are slow to learn to think in radically different terms.

But God, as always, has a better idea. And if we will find and follow His plan, we'll discover that we don't need the trappings of the mass schooling behemoth because learning is at its base, a simple and natural process. The trick is to stretch our minds to the point where they can let go of the presuppositions inculcated through our own school experiences and seek out and embrace the Scriptural ideal.

This is why I don't like the term *home school*. Home is not a school and school is not a home. Two things I don't want in my home are a skunk and a school. Oh, I know we all use the term. We say *home school* but it's better to say *home education*. You can send someone to school without giving him or her an education. To school someone is to emphasize the *process*. To educate someone is to emphasize the *product*. You don't want to school your children, you want to educate them. Now, I realize that what you call the task of teaching at home doesn't determine how you go about doing it. But still I've developed an emotional hot button for the term *home school*. And even worse is the contracted form, *homeschool*. It's a self-contained contradiction in terms, like *Christian rock* or *government intelligence* or the *Honorable Senator* so-and-so. You get the picture.

So stop saying *home school* or terrible things will happen. The Curse of the Schoolist will be upon you. Somebody will come to your house in the middle of a dark and stormy night and bite you on the neck in your sleep, and when you wake up in the morning you'll look just like your third grade teacher, Miss Brine, right down to the rimmed glasses and the gray hair tied back in a bun. Don't say you haven't been warned.

To encapsulate all this, Marilyn and I have coined the term *schoolism*. We see this as the root of nine-tenths of the teaching problems encountered by home educators. The definition is a little cumbersome, but look at it and think it over a minute:

> *Schoolism is a philosophy of education based on the assumption that the things that are done in schools are, for the most part, necessary, effective, and constitute a logical response to the findings of thorough research on the process of learning.*

In other words, we assume that schools do what they do well, and that they have good reasons for the way they do it. We figure they have done a lot of research on how children learn best and designed their approach accordingly. We therefore, consciously or unconsciously, pattern our educational system at home after theirs.

But it ain't so. For example, research shows that girls mature faster than boys, and may be as much as two years ahead in emotional development at compulsory attendance age. Yet we start them in school at the same time. Research also shows that there are differing styles of learners. Yet by and large, especially in elementary and middle school, children are all taught in essentially the same way.

The fact that you are even considering home education shows that you have at least seen cracks in their veneer of authority. But perhaps you haven't gone the whole distance. That is, it may be that you have rejected school as a perfect example, but haven't reached the point of shedding the bulk of your social presuppositions and gone back to Scripture to find and apply God's plan for educating children. We know enough to know that we have a lot more to learn about God's way. We've started but not nearly finished a study in which we're reading through the whole Bible and noting every reference to learning. However, through study and through the trial-and-error experience we've had over the years, we've come across several important differences between the school method of education and God's way. These differences illustrate why it's important to learn to shed our schoolishness and use Scripture for our model. Let's look at some of them.

Tutorial Teaching Style vs. Apprenticeship Teaching Style

Schoolishness regards teaching as primarily the process of one person who knows more imparting his knowledge to one who knows less, chiefly through the use of language. The teacher is more active, the learner is more passive. I knew a mom (a former classroom teacher) who so officialized her role that she wouldn't let her children help her decorate bulletin boards. You have to have bulletin boards, you know, and they have to be perfect. So she kept the children's grubby little paws out of the project. One problem. Children learn much more by doing things than by having things done for them. Another lady I knew, who had been trained as a teacher but had gotten married and had children rather than pursuing her career, set up a typical classroom in her basement and really went through the routine with her one daughter. She explained that even though there were only the two of them in the room, they were in school now and things had to be done differently in school. She must raise her hand to ask a question and address her mother as Mrs. Jones rather than Mommy (this is a true story—only the names have been changed to protect the ignorant). That didn't make sense even to a first grader and, thankfully, didn't last long.

Both of those examples are pretty extreme, but I'm trying to illustrate how we tend to adopt images in our minds of the way things are *supposed to be* without reasoning out what is the most productive way of doing things.

In contrast to the tutorial style, consider the apprenticeship style. Christians use the word *discipleship* and that fits pretty well. If we realize that the family is the

Chapter 2 **Doing It God's Way**

purest form of discipleship, we've come a long way toward good child training. Apprenticeship, by whatever term it's called, has been used for centuries as a method of career training and in fact it's the way we learn how to do most of the important things we do in life. We watch another person do things, try doing them ourselves, and communicate with him as he demonstrates and coaches us.

Jesus was the master teacher of all time and this is exactly the method He chose, along with a host of great leaders in Scripture. As Moses did with Joshua, and Elijah did with Elisha, Jesus picked out His disciples and involved them in doing what He was doing as He coached them, giving them increasing degrees of freedom and responsibility as they were ready.

> MARK 3:14 *He ordained twelve **that they should be with** Him, and that He might send them forth to preach...* KJV (emphasis mine)

Thus He prepared the men who soon would turn the world upside down.

Had those guys lived in our day, they would have been taken out of the scene of action—the local church and community—and sent away to seminary. Today we school preachers, we don't disciple them.

Home education should be looked at not as a variation of institutional school, but as an apprenticeship in living. Don't try to create a school in your home and emulate your past teachers; emulate Jesus by involving your children in the business of daily life, giving them gradual increases of responsibility and freedom as they progress and teaching them the information they need as the needs arise.

23

Doing It God's Way Chapter 2

Learning For Doing vs. Learning By Doing

School is a place, generally speaking, where children go to learn. They don't go there to use the knowledge, just to obtain it. I recognize there are exceptions to this, such as technical or vocational schools where products or services are actually produced by the students in the process of learning, but they're comparatively few and far between. in the average elementary or middle school, children attend to learn, not to do. Compare a school to a factory: In the factory, learning happens all the time. Every employee starts out knowing less about the factory's operation and his role in it than he will know even in a few hours or days. He does his learning in the process of producing the shoes or automobiles or trash bags the factory makes. In a school, learning happens also. But the knowledge obtained is divorced from its place in the natural scheme of things. I think this is a big part of the reason that school has become such a game. Students, even the bright ones, learn to play games because they know that the reward for achievement comes not when they demonstrate their knowledge by using it to produce a real product or service, but when they meet the challenge of filling in answer blanks correctly. It's like football practice in that the students go through certain routines during the week and then play the big game on Friday. The difference is that they tend to forget much of the material in question because they know they'll be facing a different kind of game at the end of next week, for which they will need to know a different set of plays.

Chapter 2 **Doing It God's Way**

Although high school offers a bit more opportunity for specialization and for application of knowledge through shop classes and the like, it still falls far short of providing the learning opportunities in the real world. For instance, when I was in high school I took a course in American government. I don't remember much of what I heard because I had a very boring teacher and I couldn't see any particular need for the information.

My children, on the other hand, are involved in the real business of government. My eldest son was elected chairman of our county's Republican party at the age of nineteen. That was a milestone in his political activity, but not the beginning of it. He traces his interest back to the presidential election of 1980 when he was six years old. I mentioned to the family one evening that I was about to walk down to the neighbor's house for a few minutes to catch the TV news about the election (we have never had a television). My sons asked me who the good guy was and I told them that I favored Reagan over Carter, thus making Reagan a hero at our house regardless of the fact that none of the children knew the first thing about him. Rickey had already demonstrated a strong interest in history and government, having read the A Beka fourth grade history book cover to cover eight times before the end of first grade. From that time on he read history books, newspapers and political magazines as fast as he could get his hands on them. This led to working as a volunteer in local elections when he was still so young he had to hitch a ride to headquarters for lack of a driver's license. Now twenty, he has seen his interest in politics spread to his brothers and sisters as well as a number of friends. In the past couple of congressional elections no less than six of my children, down to age nine worked answering phones at headquarters, passing out literature, manning the polls and whatever. Some of them go to the state nominating convention with me each year, write letters to the editor, help with county party functions, etc. There's a lot of difference between the way I learned about government and the way they did it. I learned it in a classroom, isolated from the real thing. They learned about it in the process of doing the job. Their teachers were the work itself; their textbooks were political magazines, educational radio programs, their fellow party workers, leadership seminars, and other sources of input. Compare that to the opportunities in the average high school, where the closest thing to real government is the chance to run for student council.

Children in school write letters that no one reads except a teacher who does so only to rate the letter on how well it is written. Children in the real world write letters to the editor that influence community sentiment, to legislators to influence government policy and to other real people about real matters. Their letters get read and usually answered.

Children in school learn mathematics in order to pass tests. Children in the real world learn mathematics to manage home businesses and balance checkbooks. That's just one more example of the difference between school learning and real-world learning. Learning that is used sticks in the mind. Learning that serves no immediate purpose except to advance through the learning system is quickly forgotten once the hurdle of the test is surmounted. Knowledge: use it or lose it.

Chapter 2 Doing It God's Way

Earlier is Better vs.
Purposes and Seasons

In his book, *Better Late Than Early*, Dr. Raymond Moore analyzed a number of scientific studies indicating clearly that school attendance is better delayed until eight or ten or even twelve years of age, based on emotional, intellectual, and physical reasons. Despite the availability of such evidence education unions are constantly calling for earlier compulsory attendance ages and more money for early childhood programs such as Head Start. The reasons for their agitation have nothing to do with the welfare of children. Earlier attendance creates jobs for more teachers, pumps more money into school systems and pulls children out of their homes for more of their early years, making it easier for social engineers to break down their ties to family and influence them in desired attitudes.

At the same time some educators, not aware of research findings to the contrary (you don't think they teach them that sort of heresy in teachers' colleges, do you?), honestly believe that the earlier children begin their structured academics, the more successful they'll be. In harmony with this idea is the companion assumption that in order to reach a desirable level of knowledge by graduation time a student must not only start early, but also keep up a certain consistent pace of learning.

Pioneer home-education advocate John Holt likened this theory to a railroad timetable. If you were starting out in City A at 8:00AM and wanted to be in City E by noon, then you would have to reach the intervening cities of B, C and D at the times called for in the timetable or you'd be late arriving in City E. This, he points out, assumes that the train travels at a fairly consistent rate of speed. And while that may be true of trains, it is not true of learning. Children learn, Holt said, not at a steady lifelong rate but in spurts. School timetables may be useful and even necessary in mass education, but at home it's a different ballgame.

> ECCLESIASTES **3:1** *To every thing there is a season, and a time to every purpose under the heaven.* KJV

Home educators would be wise to stop trying to live up to the expectations indicated by packaged curriculum materials or teachers' guides and start learning how to connect God's purposes with God's times. I recall being taught how to keep and balance a checkbook in eighth grade at age thirteen. I passed the math course, but by the time I got my first checkbook five years later, I had long since forgotten anything I had learned on the subject. I had wasted time and effort back there in junior high school, and deepened my distaste for mathematics by being forced to study and take tests on something for which I had no use or interest (today I let my wife handle the checkbook).

Part of the problem in schools is that they want to teach children things they don't need to know (one text had eight pages of material on Marilyn Monroe), fail to teach things they should know (such as the principles of the Constitution and who Nathan Hale was), or teach worthwhile things but at inappropriate times.

Sex education is a good example of bad timing among other things. Thirty years ago we learned as much as we needed to know in a health or biology course. That usually took place in high school. Now we have a U.S.

Chapter 2 **Doing It God's Way**

Surgeon General who wants sex ed taught starting with kindergarten, and with no mention of moral implications. But entirely apart from morals, what do five-year-olds need with sex education? Their parents are pretty uniformly agreed that those young people have no business using what they're learning until many years hence, so why start training them in it now?

The excuse given is that children are at risk from deadly diseases and so need to understand the biology involved as early as possible. The flaw in this reasoning is that if children just refrain from high-risk behavior, their chances of contracting such an illness are very small. So the social engineers try to convince us that young people are inevitably going to act like animals and the best thing to do is train them to prevent pregnancy and disease. It seems to be their assumption that there is nothing that can be done to train young people to use self-control instead of disease-prevention measures. Or we might better say that they have no *interest* in teaching self-control. I am inclined to believe that certain people in high places are in fact trying to encourage illicit behavior and so seek to teach children things they wouldn't otherwise learn until years later, thus creating premature interest in something they are by no means emotionally or spiritually ready to handle.

This matter of readiness, I think needs careful consideration. Our mental model of school as an educational norm suggests to us that children have largely the same learning needs at the same ages, and that the textbooks are written at about the right level of difficulty for the age for which they are written. For instance, I think it's safe to say that it's generally considered "normal" for children to be in first grade at age six, and to read in that grade. But my own family demonstrates cracks in this assumption. Our oldest son, Rickey, taught himself to read at age four without phonetical instruction. Marilyn read to him a lot from infancy and he just picked up a sense of what letters made which sounds. Other parents who had a similar experience with a child have reported that when their child went to school the kindergarten or first grade teacher was angry that the child had been permitted to learn to read *early* because it upset the routine for one child to be significantly ahead of his classmates. Our son Matthew on the other hand, required a long program of instruction in phonics and didn't really take off as an independent reader until age seven. In school he would almost surely have been labeled as having some sort of learning problem. But as he was learning to read at seven he was teaching reading to his sister, five-year-old Emily. When he'd finish a phonics workbook, he would give it to Emily and say, "Here, Emmy, this is your book now." And then he'd work through it with her. By age ten, Rickey, Matt, and Emily were all excellent readers. Which age is the *right* one at which to teach reading?

Rickey was a very active (to put it mildly) boy who was always colliding with new experiences (and coffee tables) at full speed. I think he would have been very frustrated had we tried to discourage him from sounding out words at age four just because it's a little earlier than most children learn to read. Marilyn and I are both satisfied that sensitive, introspective little Matthew would have been deeply hurt had we tried to squeeze him into the "normal" mold and force him to read at six. How many millions of children have suffered the former or latter fate because they were judged by the "average" standard and saddled with a label that followed them through the rest of their schooling and possibly the rest of their lives?

Along with readiness, a second key to timing is need. (I know. My experience with checkbook balancing is a prime example.) Apparently I was ready to learn the information as far as ability was concerned, but I had no present need to know and so no occasion to use what I had learned. Not for five years, anyway. By the time I had a need to know, I had forgotten the information. Use it or lose it.

This is not to say that you shouldn't let your child learn about things in which he's interested just because he has no immediate need to know them. If your child finds it interesting to read about whaling or piracy, I see no need to discourage him from reading on the subjects just because he doesn't have an imminent prospect of employment in either profession. What I'm saying is that I think we need to consider it carefully before *requiring* a child to learn something he has no present need to know. In some cases, I don't think it would hurt anything, such as studying geography. In other cases, I suspect there could be harm of a greater or lesser degree. For instance, I see no need to require a girl to study calculus at fifteen if she and her parents feel that her career calling is to be a homemaker. Her time could be better spent studying more domestic subjects such as cooking or helping manage the family business. If at age twenty it appears that she is going to need calculus after all, she's hardly too old to learn it.

In the home-education community, as in most social circles, people seem to be very impressed with children who reach educational goals earlier than is normally expected, such as finishing a high school curriculum at age ten. Personally, I think most healthy ten-year-olds, taught at home by diligent parents, could accomplish that. But what's the point? We've so exalted the artificial and materialistic *system* of schooling in our society that it now constitutes a false economy. Grades are its currency, with A's being more valuable than B's, C's more valuable than D's, and so on. Diplomas and degrees represent various levels in the social pecking order, with those who have neither forming the lowest caste. But all this is Monopoly money where the rubber meets the road. It is much less important to ask how far along in school your child is at age ten, than how dedicated and productive he is in service to God and man at age twenty. I know a Christian counselor on the staff of a local church who went to college for five years but didn't graduate because he was after an education rather than a degree. He never has received a degree, but he stays booked weeks in advance with counseling appointments because he knows how to give people effective, Biblical answers to their problems. And most of those answers weren't learned in a classroom but in the prayer closet and the laboratory of life.

Benjamin Franklin is one of my educational heroes and was one of the stellar players in the founding of our country. He only attended school two years in his life, yet gave himself a superb education by dealing with his educational needs as they arose and following his interests. In school he had proved himself excellent in reading, fair in writing, and poor in arithmetic. When his father could no longer afford school tuition he brought Ben home at the age of ten to work in the family shop making soap and candles. Later he was apprenticed to his brother, a printer. During his teen years and on throughout life, Franklin read voraciously. He wrote newspaper articles and studied a British journal called *The Spectator* to improve his style. As a boy he scrimped to buy books and taught himself algebra, geometry, navigation, grammar, logic, and natural and physical sciences. He studied French, German, Italian, Spanish, and Latin. He established the first subscription library in the world, the first city hospital in America, the newspaper that became the *Saturday Evening Post* and the academy that evolved into the University of Pennsylvania. At the end of his life he was world renowned as a statesman, scientist, diplomat, author, philosopher, inventor, publisher and educator. Washington and Jefferson were among his admirers, as was just about everybody else in the country at the time.

The point I want to make about Franklin is that (in addition to following his interests) the key to his very effective education was in satisfying his need to know. A little-known anecdote that illustrates this is the story of a time when young apprentice Ben was left to run the office one afternoon in the absence of brother James. A lady came in to place a print order and Ben realized that he didn't have the proper math skills to take care of her. After she had left Franklin resolved to improve his mathematics knowledge so as not to be handicapped in the future. He went out, bought an arithmetic book and taught himself what he needed to know.

This was Franklin's way. He would see a need in himself (or a friend or a customer or a city) and go to work to find out what he needed to know in order to meet the need. This is not to say that children shouldn't ever study things for which they have no immediate recognizable need, for knowledge builds on knowledge and there's nothing wrong with amassing a good variety. None of us has a crystal ball and knows exactly what needs will arise when. But we mustn't lose sight of the value and effectiveness of focusing on the meeting of needs as a key to God's leading in our learning. A powerful factor in learning is motivation, and the basis of motivation is the usefulness of the knowledge.

Another example of this idea is an incident in the life of George Washington Carver, the great scientist who started life as a slave. While teaching at Tuskeegee Institute, Carver saw the need of southern farmers to develop an alternative cash crop to replace cotton as the economic staple of the South. Cotton depleted the soil badly and the boll weevil plague was slowly moving east from northern Mexico, destroying cotton crops and bankrupting farmers. Those who stayed in the cotton business seemed doomed to disaster. So Dr. Carver went to work traveling through the South, lecturing and persuading farmers to plant peanuts instead and sweet potatoes, which enriched the soil instead of wearing it out. But now the farmers were faced with barns full of peanuts and inadequate markets. One night while out walking, Dr. Carver was accosted by a drunken white farmer who threatened to kill him for having induced people to grow a crop for which there were no buyers. Carver's response was to head immediately back to his laboratory, where he locked himself in, had meals brought to him, and spent a solid week, day, and night experimenting with peanuts. The results were spectacular, and before his career ended George Washington Carver had developed hundreds of uses for the lowly peanut, ranging from peanut butter and peanut milk to shoe polish and mock chicken. He once served a meal to some visitors to the school, of which every dish was made of peanut products, right down to the ice cream he gave them for dessert.

As you go about educating your children, you will find that you get more recognition if they achieve educational goals earlier than people expect. But resist the temptation to cater to that. Recognize that each child is an individual and keep readiness and need to know in mind.

Peer-Oriented Social Development vs. Family-Oriented Social Development

By the time I was of driving age, I was thoroughly peer dependent. My parents were divorced, my siblings and I didn't get along well and we all had our circle of friends without much overlap between them. We had not much of a family life. In my senior year in high school I managed to practically live at school five days a week through classes, sports, debate events, and school plays. On weekends I spent little time at home, preferring to run around with my friends.

At the time I was pretty satisfied with my lifestyle. My schedule was centered around school and extracurricular activities, with the only real drawback being the fact that I had to attend classes and do some work. With that exception, the routine was fairly interesting.

It wasn't until graduation night that I discovered there was something wrong with this cozy scenario. That's when it hit me that my little world had just come apart. Never again would the two hundred kids in my graduating class be together again. I had learned to view my identity as a member of that group and the group had just ceased to exist.

My experience was perhaps a bit more defined than that of most of my classmates because most probably had more of a family life than I did. But we all shared some degree of peer dependency and I suspect that today, with the much higher divorce rates, the greater percentage of working mothers and the number of children in day care, the problem is more likely worse than better. Research has demonstrated that children who spend more of their elective time with their peers than with their parents tend strongly to become peer dependent, and that results in serious consequences such as low self-esteem, lack of trust in peers, pessimism toward the future, and resistance to parental authority.

Many home educators expose their children to a degree of related danger by following the school model in providing for their social needs. In the first place, they assume that children need a lot of socializing outside the family. That's not so. It only seems so because when we were growing up we were all in school together by age group and so that seems normal. But stop and think. For every hour we spent in school, how much of that time was actually in communication with anybody? Comparatively, not much. Especially in the lower grades, we spent an awful lot of time sitting at our desks, forbidden to talk. In middle school and high school there were short breaks at the end of each hour to make our way to the next class, and more or less inter-student communication in the classes themselves. But there was little that could be considered in-depth relationship building. What's more, we were separated into our own age groups. We were young people, separated from the natural environment of exposure to adults, elderly adults, and little children.

Now we're home educators, but in the back of our minds is that picture of *normal* American social life in which children spend lots of time in age-segregated environments. So we get together at special functions so our kids will have plenty of exposure to kids their own age. That's about the last thing they need. We're not preparing them for a world in which people live in age-segregated communities, but for the *real* world where age groups constantly mix in families, workplaces, churches, neighborhoods, and a thousand different organizations. Remember, the next time you're tempted to call around and invite the whole support group to go on a field trip to the zoo, you'll have a lot more fun and much more communication with your children if you go as a family instead.

Besides the socially limiting effects of age segregation, another aspect of the schoolish social model is the lack of discrimination in the choice of companions. Schools group children by age and supposedly to a degree by ability, but not by character. The beauty of home education is that you can, to a great extent, limit your child's associates to those who will be a positive rather than negative influence. Our theme of socialization is:

> PROVERBS 13:20 *He who walks with wise men will be wise, but the companion of fools will suffer harm.* NASB

Remember all the trouble you got into as a child while in the company of your peers? The difference between the school model and the Scripture model for social development is indiscriminate versus selective companionship.

Motivation by Competition vs. Motivation by Cooperation

We live in a competitive world and children in school need to learn how to compete. So they say. That's one justification for the many ways in which little children are pitted against each other, always under pressure and vying for acceptance according to whatever artificial standard has been erected.

This philosophy makes sense until one looks a little more carefully into it. In Scripture, we're told to do our best, not for the sake of doing better than someone else, but for the sake of doing better for someone else. The greatest among you shall be your servant, Jesus said. Looking at it that way, our goal should be to learn all we can in order to better serve others. That rather stands at odds with the philosophy of judging my success by whether I perform well enough to make my competitor look bad by comparison, e.g. grades. The twelfth chapter of 1 Corinthians says in reference to believers that we are all a body, and each one a member of the body. When one member suffers, the rest of the body suffers with it. When one member rejoices, the other members rejoice with it. Does that sound like fierce competition to you?

What about making a living? Shouldn't children be taught to compete in business? After all, when there are two applicants for one job, that's competition.

Not really. It is not my responsibility to beat another man out for a job. It is my responsibility to give my best effort in whatever work I do, working as unto the LORD. It's His responsibility to give me the right job. If He wants me in a job, a million other applicants are irrelevant.

Everybody is to some degree competitive by nature and it can be harnessed in the right ways to produce a lot of good, clean fun. Some people are motivated to excellence by a drive to compete. But those who have the best quality of life are not those who define success as dying with the most toys, but who dedicate their lives to the service of God and man and give their all for unselfish motives. The Apostle Paul is a standard example. His life goal was to preach the Gospel, and he endured tremendous suffering to forward the cause. He cared nothing about competing with the other Apostles to be the big shot of the early church. In fact, he wrote to the Philippians from prison that he was aware that during his incarceration others were preaching the Gospel, some from pure motives and some hoping to cause him distress while locked up. What was Paul's response?

> PHILIPPIANS 1:18 ...*Only that in every way, whether in pretense or in truth, Christ is proclaimed; and in this I rejoice, yes, and I will rejoice.* NASB

One could list a number of famous names who achieved recognition for unselfish reasons. Ben Franklin invented the lightning rod, Franklin stove, bifocal glasses and a number of other things, but would never take out a patent on an invention because he wanted others to benefit by his work rather than to maximize his own profit.

Thomas Edison sometimes worked for days at a time with no sleep but short naps to give others the benefits of the electric light, the phonograph, and hundreds of other marvels. George Washington Carver worked his way through college doing laundry by hand in order to help former slaves educate and better themselves. The man who invented the electric streetcar (I can't recall his name) was not an electricity enthusiast, but an animal lover who so hated to see horses struggling and being injured pulling horsecars up icy hills that he went to work to create a mechanical alternative. Albert Schweitzer, medical missionary to Africa, won the 1952 Nobel peace prize for humanitarian work and used his $33,000 prize money to expand his hospital and found a leper colony.

We modern home educators have some rethinking to do. I think we've lost sight of service as a motivation for learning. Maybe that's because the teaching of history is so weak that we've forgotten the lessons from the lives of the Franklins and the Schweitzers. Maybe part of the problem is our upbringing in an entertainment-saturated society in which sports figures and movie stars make quick fortunes doing little of lasting value for others. Certainly more people today revere Elvis than Edison. But whose life was of more value? We parents need to go far beyond the artificial inducements of grades and diplomas if we want to motivate our children to greatness.

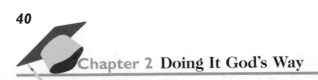

Chapter 2 **Doing It God's Way**

Academic Authority vs. Spiritual Authority

In most schools, academic knowledge is considered authoritative over spiritual knowledge. The public schools tell us that they don't want to educate the spiritual part of our children so we shouldn't worry about them learning things that conflict with our beliefs. But when you teach the history of America without regard to the spiritual lives of the characters involved you produce a caricature of history. Science without creation is not science. As for religion as an area of study, the government schools tell us that they will teach our children how to think rationally so that they can make a wise choice of the religious beliefs they feel are most meaningful to them. But of course they omit study of Christianity and teach instead the mythology of the Norse or Greeks or Romans.

God hasn't given us the privilege of choosing our religion. He's quite narrow-minded about it, in fact. He says there is only one true God and therefore only one true faith. As for natural knowledge being the key to spiritual knowledge, He has other ideas entirely. ROMANS 1:18–32 contains a fascinating description of the process by which man rejects the knowledge of God and thereby grows increasingly less capable of understanding facts. Verses 21 and 22 state the theme of the section:

> *For even though they knew God, they did not honor Him as God, or give thanks; but they **became futile in their speculations and their foolish heart was darkened.** Professing to be wise, they became fools...* (emphasis added)...

Three times the passage says that God "gave them over," first to impurity (vs.24), next to degrading passions (vs.26), and finally to a depraved mind (vs.28). The Greek word here translated depraved literally means not approved. If the goal of our study is to show ourselves *approved* unto God (1 TIMOTHY 2:15), then we shouldn't be surprised that those who reject God in learning end up *without understanding* (ROMANS 1:31).

Godliness and academic learning are not in conflict with each other. Quite the contrary, when we put God first in teaching our children, we avoid the "vain speculations" of evolution, Freudian psychology and Keynesian economics, among other falsehoods. Marilyn and I have found that the more our children internalize Scripture, the clearer and brighter their minds are for understanding and retaining academics.

Learning for Self vs. Learning for Service

We already touched on this in discussing competition vs. cooperation, but a couple of points still need mention. The school model for home education suggests that the purpose of learning is advancement of self. Apart from the competition aspect, this is a pretty selfish motivation. The world's way is to use our knowledge to raise our own standard of living by making more money, living in a better neighborhood, and having more toys. A higher standard of living is not sinful, but it becomes sinful when exalted to first place. This is why we shouldn't teach our children that the purpose of an education is to "get ahead." Ahead of what? People who have great resources of knowledge also receive a lot of admiration from others. There's nothing like a Ph.D. after one's name to command instant respect in most circles. But the down side of profuse learning is that if it is not sanctified by Godly character, it serves to make one proud (1 CORINTHIANS 8:1). And JAMES 4:6 tells us that God is opposed to the proud, while giving grace to the humble. Jesus told His followers that the greatest of them would make himself a servant to the others (MATTHEW 20:27) and that whoever wished to have life should give up his life for His sake (LUKE 9:24).

If you want to model your children's education after the principles of Jesus, teach them that the goal of learning is service.

Learning All You Can vs. God's Priorities In Learning

There's an old joke about a class clown who gave a book report on the telephone book. When called upon to speak he went to the front of the room, faced his teacher and classmates and said, *"The Smithville Telephone Book*: It has a lousy plot, but a tremendous cast of characters." Then he returned to his seat.

Somehow I doubt that he had really read that book. But if he had, he would have processed quite a bit of information through his brain. The reality is, however, that even if he had read and remembered every word, he would have accomplished practically nothing because most of the information was useless to him.

Our school system is generally weak in elucidating the various values of information. At the college level for instance, if a student is a music major preparing to teach music as a career, music appreciation is a very important course to him. It's in the center of what he has gone to college to do and what his role will be in the adult world. On the other hand, he might be required to take a physical education course that, to him, would be much less valuable. Yet the system is set up in such a way that a low grade in phys ed would lower his grade point average just as much as a low grade in music appreciation. The values built into the system do not reflect the values of real life.

While some learning is more valuable than other learning, some learning is of no value and even counterproductive. People have been granted Ph.D's after having written scholarly papers on such scientific phenomena as the Nebraska Man, a prehistoric creature once believed to be a missing link between ape and man. It wasn't considered too speculative that Nebraska Man had been reconstructed entirely based on suppositions drawn from examination of one small fossil. That fossil was later discovered to be a pig's tooth.

God actually forbids seeking certain kinds of knowledge. DEUTERONOMY 12:30 prohibited the Israelites from the study of the false gods of the nations around them. JEREMIAH 10:2 contains another prohibition on learning the ways of heathen worship. Paul wrote to the Roman church:

> ROMANS 16:19 *...I would have you wise unto that which is good, and **simple concerning evil.*** KJV (emphasis mine).

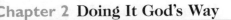

The modern counterpart of this heathen learning would be the values clarification, New Age principles, and emphasis on homosexuality as an alternative lifestyle.

To honor God's priorities in learning we have to subordinate the learning of information to the learning of character. A clue to this is found in the first chapter of Proverbs, in which wise Solomon, writing to his son, lists several purposes of the book:

> PROVERBS 1:2–4 *To know wisdom and instruction, to discern the sayings of understanding, to receive instruction in wise behavior, righteousness, justice and equity; to give prudence to the naive, to the youth knowledge and discretion...* NASB

Note that in a list of ten qualities to be learned, knowledge is ninth in order. In 2 PETER 1:5–7, Peter gives a pattern for growth in the Christian life. It starts with faith, then lists virtue, and knowledge comes third. In neither of these two lists is knowledge the writer's first concern. Character is always the foundation of learning. To educate a rebel only makes a smarter rebel.

Children as Group Members vs. Children as Unique Individuals

For the most part, schools treat children as group members. That is, they operate on the assumption that children learn best when taught in groups and when the same approach and materials are used with the whole group, rather than trying to tailor an individual approach to each child. Almost

45

any school teacher would recognize that children have different abilities, interests, talents, backgrounds and so forth, but the structure of the system usually makes it impossible for the teacher to give any child much individual attention. One publisher who produces materials that sell to both Christian schools and home educators, states as a part of their philosophy that if you walk down a third grade hallway in a school using their curriculum materials and guides, you should ideally hear a continuation of the same process coming out the doorways of the classrooms as you move down the hall. That's how regimentedly they approach education.

Home educators are learning that children can and should be dealt with as individuals, that different ones need more and less encouragement or direction or restraint. This isn't surprising in light of Scripture. PSALM 139 speaks to this. In verses 13-16 especially, the psalmist writes of how God designs each of us individually in the mother's womb and knows before birth about everything that will happen throughout every day of life. PROVERBS 22:6 speaks to individual personality in learning by reminding us to train up a child in the way he (not they) should go.

Written Evaluations vs. Verbal Evaluations

School teachers have twenty or thirty or more students in each class as a rule. For this reason, there isn't time to talk to each child individually and ascertain in that way how well he is learning. So teachers usually have to require the children to write out a lot of answers for the purpose of evaluation.

The reason this is a problem is that children, especially in the early grades, find writing a chore. They think much faster than they can talk, and they can talk much faster than they can write. So to slow down their thinking to the pace of their writing can be very frustrating.

The Bible records for us that Jesus, in training His disciples, often asked questions of the group or individuals and waited for a verbal response. There is no record of His asking them to write their answers on paper and pass it in. Why not? Because it wasn't necessary. It's also not necessary to evaluate the progress of a home taught child. Mom can assign a chapter of reading, and if she wants to know what Junior has learned, she has only to ask him. If the text book contains review questions at the end of a section or chapter, there's no need to require him to write the answers out. If those questions are worth asking, they're worth discussing. Ask him to orally tell you how he would answer the question. To make him write out answers that he could give orally in a fraction of the time is an exercise in futility. It suggests to the student, and especially the young child whose motor skills are least developed, that writing is a great drudgery with little real use.

The question often arises, *If I don't make my child respond to questions in writing, how will he get enough writing practice?* The answer is simple. I'll give it to you in a later chapter.

A Final Word

I'm sure this list of differences between the school model and the Scripture model is by no means complete. Nor is it in any particular order. Its purpose is to call your attention to the fact that there's a tremendous difference between God's principles for learning and the policies of the mass-education system of our day. Hopefully, it will help you as a home educator to open your mind and look for the best ways to teach your children rather than falling into a routine that is comfortable because it's familiar.

*Train up a child
in the way he should go:
and when he is old,
he will not depart from it*

—PROVERBS 22:6 KJV

Chapter 3
Starting Right, Staying Right.

NO BUILDING IS ANY MORE STABLE than its foundation. Remember Jesus' parable about the two houses? One man built his house upon the rock. The rain fell, testing the roof. Then the wind blew, testing the walls. Then the floods burst against it, testing the foundation. The house stood. It had passed the test. The man's neighbor, Joe Schlock, built his house upon the sand. Along came another storm. When last seen, Joe was perusing the classifieds looking for an apartment.

What was the difference between the two houses? The only structural factor we're told about is the foundation—bedrock in one case, sand in the other. Survival depended on the quality of the foundation. That's why we consider the preceding chapter so important. It's when parents build on something other than the foundation of Biblical principles that their childrearing doesn't produce the fruit they hope for.

Because our experience with home education has been so positive, Marilyn and I were a little confused for the first few years as we watched other families start teaching their children at home and later give it up and put them back in school. A lot of other families started and stayed with it, but seemed to find the whole thing a burden. A newsletter we received one January from an area support group carried an article that started out, "Well, the Christmas holidays have come and gone and now it's time to blow the dust off the books and get back to the old grind..." Our reaction was, what grind?

The problem is that people have built on the wrong foundation. Their home-education programs have fallen or at least warped under the winds of stress because

Chapter 3 **Starting Right, Staying Right.**

they weren't built on the right philosophy. Most of the parents we know who have put their hand to the plow and then turned back, did so because of hassles they could have avoided had they started out on the right foot. One of the biggest blessings we get in our ministry is seeing a face in a seminar audience go in seconds from an expression of tension and confusion to one of profound relief. This often happens when a concept is explained that shows how self-made problems can be remedied by a simple change of approach.

This chapter, combined with the one before it, is our philosophy of home education in a nutshell. We have put our views into the form of five suggestions based on our observations throughout fourteen years of home educating and helping others home educate. If you can learn to apply the principles explained (they aren't complicated) here we don't expect you to have much trouble with the teaching-learning process. So how do we go about building a home-education program on a solid foundation? I'm glad you asked.

Suggestion #1 Clarify Your Motives

As I mentioned earlier, there was a time when I encouraged everybody to home educate. Even if they had hesitations about the concept or their ability to handle the job, I figured if they'd try it they'd see the advantages and stick with it. Besides, I reasoned, it couldn't help but be good for the children to escape the peer pressure and other negative influences of school.

I long ago reversed myself. Although I still think kids are better off out of school, I've learned to think in terms of the whole movement rather than just individual families. While home educators have made great strides in gaining social acceptance and legal freedom for our lifestyle (why does that term make me uncomfortable?), we still have a long way to go. For that reason, we can't afford the baggage of families who don't put their best effort into the job. Our detractors are eagerly looking for more examples of people who confirm their impression of us as knuckle-draggers with room temperature IQ's. Our only refutation for them is success.

> PROVERBS 27:11 *Be wise, my son, and make my heart glad, that I may reply to him who reproaches me.* NASB

That means that parents who opt for home education should, for the sake of other families as well as their own, be willing to put out some effort. We're not talking qualifications, but rather commitment.

You might be surprised at how many people plunge into home education with very little consideration of what's involved. Some of the reasons we hear are pretty weak:

It's different.

Difference for the sake of difference makes no more sense than sameness for the sake of sameness. Yet some people take up home education for the same reason others buy exotic pets such as ocelots and boa constrictors. Pretty thin. Yet the opposite is sometimes true.

Chapter 3 **Starting Right, Staying Right.**

It's in vogue.

Home education is new to most of our society, but it's coming into fashion and now it's as if some consider it a mark of style. There are certain things you must do if you want to ride the wave of fashion and home education is one of them. In Christian circles, you're just not up to spiritual snuff if you let someone else teach your children. That's outmoded. Join the ranks of the spiritual yuppies.

It's cheaper.

This at first seems to be a rather unworthy sentiment when you consider that it is the welfare of our children we're talking about. Still, it makes more sense than either of the previous two reasons. When asked by a prospective home educator for a guideline, we say that you can teach your children at home for a year spending only about as much as you would spend on tuition in a private Christian school for a month. You still need more meaningful reasons than this if you would be a successful parent teacher. It doesn't reflect the necessary commitment to spiritual and academic excellence.

If these three attitudes typify your interest in home education, then you're building on sand. But the answer isn't to write off the idea altogether. Instead, look a little deeper into the matter and you'll find that there are excellent reasons to forge ahead:

It's a Biblical principle.

I've been challenged on this and I can't find a verse of Scripture that says "Thou shalt not send thy child to school". But I have observed that every time the Bible records a command to teach something to children, the command is directed to the parents and sometimes, to the grandparents as well. I haven't been able to find a single exception in Scripture. You may not consider that an ironclad case, but the pattern is strong enough for me.

More and better time with your children.

When our daughter Gracie was two years old she was beginning to learn the rudiments of doctrine from some little books her mom read to her. One day as Marilyn and some of the children were driving along in our van, my wife heard little Gracie's voice in prayer from behind her: "Dear Deedee (she hadn't quite learned to pronounce 'Jesus' yet), please come into my heart. But not my tummy. Or I would frow up." Gracie could have been in a day care center that day, but she wasn't. Nor were her older brothers and sisters in school. They were all either at home or elsewhere, engaged in the business of our family. That's why we have been blessed with so many delightful memories such as Gracie's grappling with theology. We could farm our children out as do the majority of other parents in our society, but look what we'd miss. Along with the funny and winsome happenings of childhood, parents who spend much time with their children have the pleasure of sharing in their discoveries and accomplishments. Why send your child off to school when he's right at the age when most children crack the code that unlocks the wonders of the written word? What a shame to miss the fascinating process of learning to read or count or use an encyclopedia. Sure, you could say that there's time for some of this after school, but why settle for a crust when you can have the whole pizza? Besides, children often come home from school sick of books and papers and with

Chapter 3 **Starting Right, Staying Right.**

homework yet to do. (Studies show, by the way, that children who do homework, especially with involvement on the part of their parents, tend to excel in academics.) My suggestion is to make it all homework. Just pitch the schooling.

Children naturally develop a deep respect for those who teach them. To deflect that privilege to a stranger seems the same as selling one's birthright for a mess of pottage.

Individualized instruction.

The teacher in a school classroom is at an automatic disadvantage. She has twenty or thirty or more children with varying degrees of need and ability in different subjects of study. She can't give any child much individual attention without neglecting others, hence the self-explanatory form of most text materials. A high degree of standardization is necessary, which means that individual needs are often lost in the shuffle. At home this isn't the case. Mom has only one or two or a few children in the classroom and she can therefore give more time to each one. She also is in a position to know what special needs for encouragement, restraint, or prodding are a part of each child's personality. Teachers necessarily spend a lot of time and energy in just getting to know their students, especially early in the year. Not so with moms. They all have those antennae, you know.

> PROVERBS 22:6 *Train up a child in the way he should go, even when he is old he will not depart from it.* NASB

57

We usually emphasize the "not depart" portion of the verse, which is very important. But don't overlook that little phrase, "the way he should go." Literally, it would be better expressed, *in his way*. We are to train a child according to his individual bent. Children have differing abilities and learning styles, and those things may be comprehended by some school teachers but will surely be overlooked by others. At home, Mom and Dad can learn to discern such factors and plan curriculum, methods, and activities accordingly. Just as some children aren't college material, although they are just as bright as others, differences exist in other aspects of learning as well. The individualized program parents can develop for each of their children is the best and most natural guarantee that a child will not become a square peg in a round hole later on.

Spiritual growth.

Not all home educators demonstrate by their children's character that they have done a competent job of Christian parenthood. But the tools and materials for building Godliness in a child are more readily available at home than anywhere else. Though in our day it is accepted practice to delegate spiritual training to Sunday schools and Bible clubs, God places the responsibility on parents.

I suspect one reason for that is that in our homes we're more accountable. My family knows when I am spiritually cold even if I have church friends and others fooled completely. And Mom and I know our children's weaknesses, too. Outsiders may see little but the positive side of our offspring, but we know their sin nature.

Chapter 3 **Starting Right, Staying Right.**

The key advantage of home is that it can be a spiritual greenhouse. Plants don't have to live in a greenhouse all their lives, but those who start out there have the assurance that they won't be exposed to the destructive outside elements before they have grown to the strength and maturity necessary to survive. I've heard a number of people espouse the idea that the way to teach children to stand alone is to throw them out of the nest and let them fight it out in the coliseum from early on. May I say I am appalled at just how stupid that idea is. Any animal on the upper end of the food chain has the sense to protect and train its young through intense personal contact until they can do the things that the adults of the species do. Imagine a lioness deserting her half-grown cubs to hunt zebras on their own. They'd get their teeth kicked out. But we do that very thing when we send our young children to school. We force them to face social pressures that in some ways are greater than those of the adult world. Do we really expect them to stand alone in the company of who-knows-whose kids? At five years of age?

Back home in the greenhouse, we have the inestimable advantage of being able to control the environment. We can give our children the spiritual nurture and instruction they need, then when they need the challenge of exposure to more of the outside world, we can lead them, rather than throw them out into it. Children in school have the advantage of exposure to many different spiritual influences. Home-educated children (if their parents are wise) have the greater advantages of exposure to predominantly healthy spiritual influences and the example of their parents in responding to them. A comparison could be made between these two approaches to spiritual training and two models of swimming instruction. Home education, in the spiritual aspect, is like leading your child down the beach and into deeper and deeper water as he gains the skills and confidence he needs. It's a gradual thing, with Mom or Dad holding on as much as needed until by degrees the child learns to swim well enough so that the depth of the water is irrelevant. Sending children to school, especially at tender ages, is like pushing them off the dock into deep water and high waves. They must either sink or swim, and even those who manage to swim sometimes swallow enough water to do them permanent damage.

Academic success.

Nationally, home education is proving itself to be the superior method of teaching children. Many, many studies have been done that demonstrate this and our powerful competitors in the educationist unions have been unable to refute it. A good example that surfaced a few years ago was a report from Alaska comparing home education with public schooling. Because of the tremendous distances between population centers and the sparseness of the rural population in our largest state, the public education system has provided to many families in remote areas the same text materials for use at home as are used in the schools. Here, where many families have home taught their children traditionally out of necessity, the superiority of home instruction over public school has found perhaps its clearest example. The home-educated children scored considerably higher on their achievement tests than did their schooled counterparts even though they were taught from the same books. And of course the educational level of the parents was lower than that of the public school teachers, nearly all of whom have college degrees and certification.

No peer dependency.

Americans have been talking about the *generation gap* for—well, for generations. What we mean by the term is that in our society, there has come to exist a fairly well-defined line of demarcation between the lifestyles of one generation and another. In my adolescent years, primarily the sick sixties, the gap seemed quite pronounced. There was young people's music and old people's music. Young people's lingo and old people's lingo. In dress, manners, entertainment and interests, we were as different as night and day from our parents.

That divorcing of the generations by each other was unnatural. What researchers seemed to just be coming to realize was that it was only one side of a coin, the other side of which was equally unnatural. We were unnaturally dependent on each other as young people and it was that fact that caused us to resist absorption into the adult world. We had been separating the generations—by the use of schools, day care centers and retirement homes—long enough for that separation to distill into exclusion. I've heard protests that some studies show that the strongest influence on school children comes from their teachers. I'm not well versed in research, but that doesn't ring true with my own experience in school. By the time I was a teenager, it was my peers, not my teachers, who dictated what I wore, what music I listened to, and what activities I spent my time in. It was socially unacceptable to respect older people just because they were older, and considered rather dashing and noble to resist authority.

Home education gives the parent control over the factors that once made peer dependency almost a given. Parents and children spend much more time together and communicate more during that time. The amount of time children spend with their age peers and with which ones it is spent, is under the control of the parents; whereas otherwise it would be at the discretion of the school system, with little if any regard to character matters. In things social, as well as in things spiritual, home education is the opportunity for parents to provide their children with healthy associations and protect them from the harmful.

Values transferral.

You can tell an awful lot about a person by knowing what he desires and whom he admires. Another good reason to teach your children at home is that it gives you much more influence over the development of their values.

Though it's happened many times, I'm still shocked when I look into a teenager's bedroom and see the walls decorated with posters of rock music stars. Nowadays, of course, one can see purveyors of so-called Christian rock on such posters, their appearance and stage behavior indistinguishable from that of their secular counterparts. Observers such as those in the news media, who have tracked these musical paragons in their personal lives, have reported that as a group they are insecure, tense, neurotic, narcissistic, fearful, and immoral. Frequent suicides and fatal drug overdoses in their ranks speak eloquently of the despair that accompanies dissolute and perverted lifestyles.

Chapter 3 **Starting Right, Staying Right.**

Yet millions of our young people tack their graven paper images to their bedroom walls and worship them daily as heroes. It's a sad commentary, but it speaks volumes in telling us what young people admire.

And what do the youth of America desire? I don't know what the surveys say, but by my observation their wants are pretty materialistic and shallow. Popularity, nice cars, fashionable clothes, the latest CD's. Lots of freedom and leisure time, a minimum of work and responsibility.

Where do these kids get such values? Not usually from their parents. Certainly not from their parents' instruction, even if the accompanying example doesn't match well. Most moms and dads I know place value on work and achievement, morals and character. I've seen Christian parents in particular, people with high standards of character and conduct, have their hearts broken by the behavior of their sons and daughters. Parents who weathered storms, who stuck together when their marriage was under stress for the sake of the LORD and their children and each other, have watched, devastated as their adult children go through divorce almost casually. Almost proverbial is the scenario in which parents work themselves nearly into the grave to provide better material things for their kids only to see their wealth squandered by ungrateful young spendthrifts.

These evidences of wrong values have happened in all sorts of families from all sorts of backgrounds. Today it is arguably as bad as it's ever been, yet hopeful signs are appearing in home-education circles. More and more parents are keeping their children out of the bubbling cauldron of social ferment that we call the peer group by keeping them out of school and providing some direction for their social life. Researchers have found that people tend to become average. That is, we tend to acquire the common personality traits of the group in which we spend most of our time. That's why home education works so well in passing down values. We can create in our homes a worthy standard, a system of beliefs about what is good and valuable and worthy.

So we've talked about motives. Some people take a fancy to the idea of home education and jump into it without really analyzing why they're doing so. But there's no need to. There are many good reasons to teach your own children, and I hope our mention of these few will help you solidify your motivation, if that's what you need. Remember, it's commitment, not credentials, that we're looking for. If you have commitment and common sense there is no reason in the world why you can't give your children an education that will prepare them not just for more of a system, but for real life.

Suggestion #2
Get Your Children Under Control

One of the most common causes of home-education burnout is undisciplined children. A mom can collect excellent books and materials, devote many hours to the program and use all her creativity in teaching her children, but if she does not have good control over them and a manageable household she is on the doorstep of insanity.

Not only is this a problem for the family in question, but it also constitutes a negative testimony for the home-education movement, for Christian families in general, and for the LORD. We desperately need to hear more teaching on this topic in our churches, along with other aspects of family life. We'll deal more thoroughly with discipline in a later chapter, but it needed to be mentioned here as a part of your preparation for and approach to home education. It's a foundation stone.

Suggestion #3
Assemble a Basic Curriculum

Assuming this is your first year to teach at home, where do you start? That depends on your savvy and confidence. You may know exactly where you're headed and be able to just shop around and put together your personalized program from book fairs and the public library. That kind of first timer is rare though, and chances are you'd like a degree of guidance from outside.

Don't let your timidity drive you into bondage, however. There are tons of people just panting to help you out, and a lot of them wouldn't mind making some money in doing so. There is far more help available than you'll ever need, so proceed with caution. You are more competent than you may think.

One option chosen by some sheepish parents is that of video home school. We like that perhaps least of all the home-education options. It smacks too much of television, for one thing. I'm not knowledgeable enough to evaluate the effect of the screen's radiation on the viewer's

65

eyes, but I have my suspicions. More importantly, my hackles rise at the thought of a child and/or parent growing dependent on that electronic box as a teacher. It's about as far from hands-on learning as you can get. For that matter, it's also about as far as you can get from real exploration of the world around us.

Remember: the essence of home education is the parent-child relationship. There is a dimension of experience available to a parent and child learning together that transcends any other arrangement for learning. Our nature is designed that way. The child's progress is inspiration for the parent and the parent's involvement is inspiration for the child. Seating your child in front of a glowing blue screen and walking off to water your begonias is not educating him.

We're also leery of correspondence schools. Their are two main reasons for that. The first is that you have to go pretty much according to their program, which denies you the freedom to individualize your approach to each child's needs. Besides that, the only means the correspondence school has of evaluating your child's progress is by having him do a lot of writing. That can be discouraging and boring, especially when the child is in the earlier years or when the material could easily be discussed with Mom verbally.

A little aside here. Remember, whatever book you're using to teach whatever subject, you must boss the book. That book was not written for your child, it was written for use in a classroom of twenty or thirty students. If little Johnny doesn't need the twenty practice problems at the end of the page, don't make him work through them. If he has demonstrated that he's ready for the next step up, let him turn the page and go ahead. On the other hand, don't feel obligated to move ahead just because the program calls for it. If Johnny isn't ready, he isn't ready. He may need more practice or just more time.

We strongly recommend that you DON'T buy teacher's guides or curriculum guides for a program. They are largely useless and can be dangerous if you try to do everything they suggest. Just buy the books and materials you want and use them as you see fit. They may know their materials, but only you know your child. At the end of the book we'll append our suggested basic curriculum list for each grade level and tell you where to get the materials. Take the responsibility to substitute, supplement, and discard materials. Any package program you buy will contain some things you don't need at all, some things that need to be supplemented with outside materials, and some things you can toss and replace with stuff you like better for that subject. Remember, you must boss the books if you want to give your child what's best for him.

Suggestion #4: Rid the Home of Counterproductive Influences

Don't get all excited, ladies—I'm not suggesting that you divorce your husbands. What I mean here is to cleanse your home of those distractions to learning that come in sheep's clothing. My favorite whipping boy is, of course, television. Never before have so many spent so much time benefiting so few. The vast majority of the programs on the tube are either sensual, occult, violent, degrading, vain or at least distracting.

Music is another cornucopia of distraction and debasement. It's easy to get bad music and hard to find good. So-called Christian rock has so permeated the selection of tapes and CD's in religious bookstores that there's little else from which to choose. I love patriotic music, thumpless Christian music, and some classical music. Unfortunately, I'm too ignorant of classical to be able to recommend much. A lot of it is depressing or lacks resolution. But don't give up. Ask all your friends about their favorite classics and somebody will turn out to be weird enough to be able to help you.

Enough has been written about the dangers of secular music to turn anyone against it, but unfortunately no one has turned against it. Be aware of what your children are listening to. And if they're young enough to influence their tastes, get good music in the house right away to start addicting them to it.

Your child may have friends who are a negative number as playmates. If so, do something about it. It often takes creativity to limit social contact without offending somebody. You may have to set a pretty strict schedule so that Johnny will be legitimately too busy when you-know-who comes over to play. If all else fails, maybe you could buy a quarantine sign and pass the rumor that your child has leprosy.

Possessions are another possible stumbling block. Some toys and pets require more time than they're worth. You may have to smash the Nintendo and give away the pet python. Or better yet, reverse that.

Suggestion #5:
Anticipate Some Obstacles

Once you've made the decision to teach your children
at home, expect success and don't settle for anything less.
Expect to improve your performance as a teacher every
year. But don't go into this with a Pollyanna outlook that
nothing could possibly go wrong, because it could. And
it will.

We've heard some stories over the years of
people who took their children out of the pressure cooker
of school and all the learning problems cleared right up.
But those stories are in the minority. Satan hates families
and he'll do everything in his power to discourage and
distract you. His goal is to get you to give up and put
your children back in school or condition you to settle for
a mediocre educational product at home. As I said in
the first chapter, home education is basically simple.
But there are a few snares that can fall across your path
from non-educational sources.

Critics

Early in our home-education experience we
sometimes allowed our enthusiasm to bubble over a bit
and sometimes shared it with the wrong people. That was
back in the days when home educators were viewed as
being in the same class with space aliens and lizard
fetishists. It didn't take long to see that not everyone
was going to share our zeal. The situation has improved
considerably as the public has begun to see that home
education is here to stay and is producing some good
results. Still, you can rest assured that you will be criticized

from time to time by family, friends, neighbors, fellow church members, and even total strangers.

Perhaps the main reason for this is what I call the Vince Lombardi syndrome. Lombardi was a famous football coach whose philosophy of defensive play was, *The best defense is a good offense.* He meant that if you could score enough points to stay ahead of the opposing team, your defensive failures could be overcome. Evidently there is a spiritual principle here. I've noticed that when a couple makes up its collective mind to invest the effort necessary to teach its children at home, some of their acquaintances immediately seem to feel threatened. It's as if they feel obligated to either consider the same commitment for their own family or rationalize it away. And it doesn't seem to be sufficient for them to convince themselves; they have to talk you out of it as well.

So it is with any conviction. If you have it and I don't, I have to either adopt it or reject it. And it's much harder to reject it with you around making me look bad. As Mark Twain said, nothing is harder to put up with than the annoyance of a good example.

Some critics of course, are entirely on your side and honestly want the best for you. In their case, you may be able to educate them about the realities of home education and put their fears to rest. The others you should just ignore, particularly those as dedicated as Mrs. Job.

You remember Mrs. Job, no doubt? Poor old Job had done nothing wrong but God had taken his wealth, his health, and his precious children. Sitting clothed with sackcloth in a pile of ashes, he was mourning and trying to understand what was happening. Along comes his dear wife, whose gift seems to be either encouragement or

Chapter 3 **Starting Right, Staying Right.**

showing mercy. Her suggestion: curse God and die. What a sweetheart.

There are Mrs. Jobs in every age. Our friend Debbie lived next door to one. Having finally conquered her hesitations and decided to teach her children at home, she shared her enthusiasm one day with Mrs. Job, who was very concerned. Later that day she invited Debbie to go out that evening for ice cream. Lovely.

We all have our idiosyncrasies and Mrs. Job's idiosyncrasy was that she never went to Dairy Queen without her mother and a copy of the compulsory attendance statute. By the time Mrs. Job and her mother were through with poor Debbie it would have taken a mop to get her up. If you think Job's wife is precious, wait until you meet his mother-in-law.

Financial Pressures

Here's a potential source of discouragement that doesn't need much explaining. It's understandably hard to give our full attention to the needs of our children when there are pressing financial needs on our minds. And of course, it's not an uncommon problem among parents of young children. Sometimes it seems that the family always grows faster than the income.

Legal Problems

It's not much fun, living behind drawn curtains. As one who has run afoul of a compulsory attendance statute, I can testify that this sort of thing can definitely distract a parent from ministering to his children. Fortunately, there are now avenues of recourse that weren't available to us. It's unlikely that you'll need them, but they're out there now. See the appendix for some sources of legal help.

Death or Illness in the Family

These times can demolish the most rigid schedule. When they come, don't try to do everything you normally do. Remember that God brings seasons into most lives during which it seems there's nothing to do but tread water until the river goes down. Don't give up on home education during these times. You'll have to adjust your way of doing things and nothing will work as well as normally, but who expects it to? Enlist some prayer warriors and do the best you can. This too will pass.

School Hangover

We started our children out learning at home and that's definitely the easiest way. If you're taking your child out of school after months or years of attendance he may exhibit some symptoms of withdrawal. I've seen it happen both ways: one child who has had a hard time with the school pressures blossoms immediately when brought home to learn; another child is traumatized for a while by the sudden change in social environment, loss of favorite extra-curricular activities or the residual effects of emotional stress he experienced while in school. At first he may not do as well in his studies, as he was while in school. Usually this clears up with the passage of time.

Hyper Activities

No, that's not a misprint. I refer to the tendency of home educators to think that the busier they are, the better they're doing. We seem as a class to have a strong tendency to equate activity with productivity. Ain't so. A man hanging wallpaper with one hand tied behind his back is no doubt quite active, but he isn't likely to get much paper hung.

By the same token, home educators are notorious (at least to Marilyn and me) for being on the go all the time, burning energy and gasoline, faithfully making an appearance at every field trip, social outing, and science fair sponsored by the local support group. Some moms spend more time on the road than at home. This just isn't productive. It's another symptom of the old schoolist syndrome: The more extracurricular activities you're involved in, the more well rounded your education is.

Every benefit has to be weighed against its cost. When you take your children on a field trip for instance, you need to assess it for the potential value and the likely cost. Is it worth spending most of the day away from home, spending an hour or two with the children strapped into safety seats, the babies missing their naps, and not having supper ready when Dad gets home? Is the trip necessary, or could you learn as much about the chosen topic by reading a book or renting a video?

I think you get the point. But in case you haven't encountered this yet, beware. You'll soon have all kinds of well-meaning friends inviting you to get together for every event imaginable. You can't home educate if you're never home.

Again, let me emphasize that the above are factors not directly related to the home-teaching process but which can have a powerful effect on it. Usually these things, when they happen, are unavoidable. It may not reassure you much to learn that there is an even wider range of possible snags that fits under the category of avoidable. But at least you can be aware of them so as to head them off at the pass.

I want to reiterate that home education, when done sensibly, is not boring, difficult, or complicated. Parents who find it to be that way, unless they are experiencing external pressures such as those listed above, are doing something wrong.

As a matter of fact I'm surprised at the number of parents who seem to feel that children are a burden in general. Marilyn says that the hours spent working with the kids are the best hours of her day. That's a contrast to a lot of moms and dads who act as if they were given children to chastise them for their sins. Surprise! The Bible says children are a blessing, not a curse. If you remember, God told Adam and Eve to be fruitful and multiply before there had ever been a sin committed. So children aren't an evidence of judgment. Admittedly, they do entail some maintenance. Laundry, for instance. But don't confuse the issue. Before the tall of man, children were already in the blueprint. It wasn't until after sin came into the world that anybody started wearing clothes. That meant laundry. Now that's what I call a curse.

Chapter 3 **Starting Right, Staying Right.**

No building is anymore stable than its foundations.

—RICK BOYER

Part 2

Hitting the Books

Chapter 4
Curriculum

T HE BUSINESS OF putting together a curriculum for your child is not as complicated as you may fear if you're new at this. Nor is it expensive. It's just a matter of common sense and the willingness to shop around a bit. Before you go shopping, however, you need to know the size of the animal you're hunting. In a college, curriculum selection is a massive undertaking. They are dealing with preparing people for professional careers of a hundred different stripes. But to give your own child a solid basic education there is not really much you need to know in order to get started. In fact you may find that the hardest part is deciding what not to buy from the vast and colorful array of materials available out there. To illustrate the degree of difference between curriculum at its most complicated and curriculum in its simplest form, think in terms of dollars. To research, plan, design, and produce curriculum for an entire college program would cost many millions. On the other hand, if Marilyn and I were starting home education with one child this year we would probably spend about two hundred dollars. That would include not only his books and other curriculum materials, but also a globe, some maps, and some of the other hardware you might like to have in the classroom. The second year would be cheaper because we would already have those non-expendable items and would only have to replace workbooks, crayons, pencils, paper, etc. Marilyn says that curriculum costs can drop steadily over the years because as the children grow older they outgrow the use of the expendable materials and grow into the use of materials that can be reused repeatedly. For instance, you will probably not often replace a biology

Chapter 4 **Curriculum**

or advanced math book due to wear. In our family of twelve children we have in fact worn out some of those books, but we're not your average family.

Anyway, you may not want to reduce your curriculum cost overall, but rather use the savings from one area to expand in another. For instance, when your child grows out of math workbooks and into the textbook-and-scratch-paper stage, you may want to continue spending the same amount of money and using the workbook allotment on some new books for the home library. Even if you were willing to increase spending, it would take some effort to spend as much on teaching your child at home as it would to send him to most private schools. In fact, you could teach your children for much less than a hundred or two per year, but we'd rather spend the money than take the time away from teaching to scramble around in attics, libraries, and yard sales collecting bits and pieces of material.

A Bit of Philosophy

When we talk about curriclum, what do we mean? The dictionary defines it as the entire program of study of a school. In home-education circles, we usually use the word *curriculum* specifically in terms of the materials we use to teach. And that's not such a bad way to look at it for starters. Most of us use a packaged curriculum to start, feeling that in so doing we have a general guideline to help keep us on track. As we grow more experienced we begin to see things in the package that we feel are redundant or unnecessary and so we do some minor stuffectomy (removal of stuff). Later on, we do more discarding and buy some materials from outside the package to replace and supplement parts of the program as we develop more educated opinions as to what each child does and does not need. As each month and year goes by, we grow more confident and depend on packaged materials less. In developing a curriculum for our child, the issue at the heart of the matter is the question, what does God want my child to learn? That's a staggering thought if you try to grip it too tightly. But don't panic. God hasn't given you a crystal ball or sent a faxed list of studies He wants your child to pursue. He doesn't expect you to be able to give a complete answer to that question from day one.

If you're starting at kindergarten level (which is by far the easiest way to do it), there's only so much your child can handle in the way of structured academics. At that age he mostly needs to be read to a lot so that he will learn early the treasures available through the written word. You may also want to start teaching him simple phonics and how to form his letters. But there's no need to push it. Five- and six-year-old children are as yet not fully developed in their visual and motor abilities and there is just no reason to strain them. Many so-called learning disabilities are the result of emotional pressure put on children who are forced to do things they aren't ready to do in the first year or two of school. Our rule in the first couple of years is to let the child do as much as he wants to do. Five-year-olds, and in fact preschoolers, will usually want to do something that looks schoolish because their older siblings are doing it. We use simple little just-for-fun workbooks for the little ones. It satisfies their desire to be like big sister and keeps them out of mischief with the felt-tip markers at the same time.

A word here about reading. There have been several books written exposing the fallacy of sightword reading. They are right. The English language is an alphabetical language, and the symbols of our alphabet stand for sounds. In Chinese the symbols of the alphabet stand for ideas. The symbol for horse is the same as for pony. In order to make all the distinctions necessary in verbal communication, ideographic languages such as Chinese need many more symbols in their alphabets than our twenty-six. I've been told that there is a Chinese typewriter in the United Nations that has five thousand keys.

The sightword systems in use in American public schools are the main reason for the decline of literacy in our country. The reason for this is that the letters of the alphabet do not, as Chinese symbols, look anything like the idea they represent. There are no clues in the shape or arrangement of letters in a word as to the meaning of the word. There was never intended to be any. The letters stand for sounds, not objects or ideas. You can see how ridiculous sightword reading is by looking at even one line of words on this page and imagining how hard it would be to memorize their meanings by how they look. Look at a sentence written in Spanish or French. How many clues can you find to the meanings of the words by the appearance and order of the letters?

Reading is the key to education and phonics are the key to reading. If a curriculum package does not use a strong phonics approach to reading, stay away from it.

Back to the question of what God wants your child to learn. What do you already know about that? You know that the fear of the LORD is the beginning of knowledge and wisdom (PROVERBS 1:7, 9:10), so Godly character comes first. Next, you know that God wants all of us to know His Word. That means reading is essential. In fact, Hebrew children in Bible times were taught to read from the Scriptures themselves. Hmm. There must be something to this theory that the content of reading is as important as the skills of reading.

You know from your own daily responsibilities that everybody needs basic mathematical skills. It's hard to cook, pay bills, or even tithe without basic arithmetic. So although we may not agree on the desirability of higher math, we can concur on the need for basic stuff.

Do you realize that we've just laid the foundation for a life curriculum? If a person has a right relationship with God, the ability to read well and basic arithmetic skills, he has the ability to educate himself from that point on if necessary. Everything that can be learned through books is accessible to the person who has those three prerequisites. History, science, higher mathematics, language, economics, government or whatever, the door to learning is now wide open. In the beginning of formal instruction, if you supply your child with these three keys, he is able—with increasing competence—to educate himself. You can rest assured you have built a solid foundation for him.

In the years that follow, God will give you insight as you need it concerning what your child needs to study. God's life program for one of your children won't be identical to His program for any of his siblings, because no two human beings are exactly alike. If they were, one of them would be unnecessary. So stay alert to God's promptings to you and your child. Use the packaged curriculum as a checkpoint, if you choose to use one, but don't let it enslave you. No package can meet the needs of all your children equally. As time goes by, your confidence will grow and you will learn to enjoy being creative.

Some Guidelines

We don't want to be too directive in telling you how to choose a curriculum. We want you to do some sifting and decide what looks best to you. Besides, curriculum publishers are changing and revising their products all the time, and if we recommend a program as the best thing we're aware of now, that could change drastically in five years. But we do have some general ideas we'd like you to keep in mind as you begin to look around and begin to acquaint yourself with what's out there.

Choose a curriculum
that looks interesting to you

If your materials aren't interesting to you, you can rest assured that they won't be interesting to your children. I am particularly wary of programs that use a lot of workbooks where I would normally expect hardbound textbooks. These workbooks are simple to use and make the child very self-directed so that there is less work for Mom in the classroom. But that's a minus, not a plus. Mom needs to be as involved as possible in the learning process of her children because of the spiritual/emotional relationship they need to have with her. Remember, the essence of home education is the parent-child relationship.

Only a few years ago these workbook programs were very plain looking. They looked so little like the text materials we used that I could spot them a mile away. They looked as if they had been put together by the lowest bidder. But of late those producers seem to have discovered that they're competing with some very professional publishing operations and have added class to the act through the acquisition of some good graphics people and more advanced printing technology. They don't stick out like a sore thumb anymore, so beware of judging too much by appearances.

The root problem of these materials still remains. Their format is read the paragraph, answer the questions. Read the paragraph, answer the questions. It's the epitome of the problem of making question-answerers of our children rather than question-askers. The illusion is created that a student has completed a thorough course of study by filling out a series of these workbooks, but that is far from the truth. Having read one or two really good science texts is a far cry from knowing all one needs to know about science. And these workbooks are, comparatively, a long way from being really good texts. The child who has worked through one will have received a lot of right answers because of the simplicity of the layout, but he won't have been inspired to formulate questions of his own. And after all, what is learning but the quest to satisfy curiosity? It should be an ongoing process of learning how much we don't know, and stoking our hunger to find out.

Watch for the appropriate use of color

God put a lot of color in nature. It's as if He were trying to get our attention. In the younger years especially,

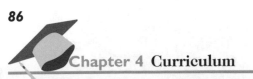

color is important in learning materials. Especially in such things as science and history, it makes a tremendous difference in the attractiveness and effectiveness of illustrations. For instance, imagine black-and-white underwater photos. Or black-and-white reproductions of paintings of Civil War battles. You can't judge a book by its cover, and neither can you judge it by its illustrations entirely. But they do make a difference.

Stay away from curriculum guides

Marilyn is adamant in warning beginning home educators against the use of curriculum guides, teacher's manuals, or whatever name these types of publications go by. If you buy a curriculum package from a publisher they will usually include one of these, sometimes at extra cost. They are a set of instructions for the use of the materials in the package and they are largely useless and even detrimental in home education.

The reason for this is that nearly all Christian text materials are written for use not in homes but in schools. Sometimes the publisher makes a conscious effort to create stuff for home educators, but generally they don't understand how learning works at home. They are school people, trained and experienced in the mass-education environment. Home is a totally different ball game. So don't even get the curriculum guide if you can avoid it, and if you do get it ignore it. It will tell you to do a lot of things that serve a purpose in the institutional classroom but make no sense at all in the home.

You may look over a brochure advertising a curriculum and come to the conclusion that you would need a teacher's manual to use it because it looks so complicated. If it's that complicated, you don't want it. Learning is simple and natural. If the program makes it no longer simple, it will make it unnatural.

How means more than what

The most important thing about your curriculum, even more important than what you use, is the issue of how you use it. I know a missionary family in Mexico who home educated their children using one of the very workbook-oriented programs I mentioned with such disapproval above, yet did a superb job. Why? Because they did their work well. In my opinion, the "tools" they bought in their curriculum package were inferior. But they supplemented them with better tools and used all their materials with skill, staying close to their children and showing interest in what they were doing. Considering that almost any home-education curriculum system can be utilized in less than three hours a day, there is plenty of time left for supplemental work in the form of additional reading, learning projects, and the like.

Don't create a system that worships system

Your child's life goal is not to stay in school forever. He will one day have to take on something other than study as a full-time occupation; he will have a home and family; and a number of other responsibilities. He will, in short, be living as a responsible adult in the real world. Our modern system of education seems to forget that fact in the elementary and secondary years, and treat children as if the only important thing they had to prepare for was more schooling.

As evidence of this, consider the area of mathematics. The tendency nowadays is to push the principles of algebra and geometry on children as early as elementary school. There might be some justification in this if it were possible to know at that age that all the children using the particular math program in question were bound for college and college-level math someday. But that isn't the case. Most of those children will not need algebra and geometry as adults. Most of them won't even need a college degree. So why do we cram such studies into them? Because we as a society have accepted the assumption that longer institutionalization is always better. We seem to feel that everybody should go to college, therefore everybody should prepare for college.

But what we are doing in fact is preparing people for something that won't happen to a lot of them, and in the process we burn up time and energy that would be better invested otherwise. We're trying to avoid that in our family.

I hated math in high school, partly because of this very problem. The disaster of "modern math" had just swept into fashion, and all the talk about sets and subsets and all that other Martian language made no sense and served no purpose I could see. Of all the senseless, boring things I had the displeasure of meeting in high school, that math course was the epitome. What they did not try to teach us in that course was any practical use for mathematics. Unlike the arithmetic texts in junior high school, there were no story problems that gave a context to the skills we were studying. I can't remember the instructor ever trying to explain to us why we were studying the material.

Marilyn, on the other hand, was a good math student. She made good grades in such horrific things as algebra and geometry. But she has never had a need to use what she learned and so she has forgotten it. If any of our children ever need those subjects, Marilyn will have to go back to the books and do a lot of re-learning in order to be able to help them. She takes a very dim view of such subjects as general requirements. They looked very impressive on her transcript, but were useless to her outside of school. The pursuit of such subjects in the educational system prepares children for more of the system, but, except for those few who end up in math-oriented careers, it does not prepare them for life.

The time spent teaching "higher" math, which most people don't need, would be better spent on practical math, which most people do need, and which few master. We have given our children a course called consumer math that deals with functions that almost everybody needs to perform. Our book teaches the student how to set up books for a small business, how to fill out IRS forms, the ins and outs of home mortgages, how to figure unit prices at the grocery store, how to balance a checkbook, and so on. These are much more commonly needed skills than how to figure the cubed root of a cross-eyed Peruvian integer or whatever those geniuses do. Some math programs prepare students for more of the school system, some prepare them for life.

Another good example of worshiping the system is the practice of writing papers. As I've said elsewhere, I believe children need to be taught to express themselves clearly in speech and in writing. But some people take this too far. They have their children spend hours writing reports and theses that nobody will ever read, when they could have spent the same amount of time learning something interesting and helpful. Why do they do this? They're preparing their children for college. In college there will be lots of term papers to write so the kids must learn to write them now so their *grades* won't suffer. Remember, grades are the currency of the false economy of the school system.

I still maintain that the best training for writing is writing things that somebody will read for the content, not to evaluate the form. List several project options and let the student choose two or three for the month. Choices might include a letter to the editor, a letter to a legislator, an inquiry to a chamber of commerce, a request for information from a historical society or institution, a report on some scientific issue for the younger siblings to study, or an article for submission to a magazine. My thirteen-year-old daughter publishes her own newsletter. It doesn't take a lot of creativity to think of more vehicles for written expression than writing term papers just for the purpose of learning how to write term papers. Assign term papers if you want a system that will prepare your child for more of the system. Assign real writing if you want to prepare him for the real world.

Respect the seasons of learning

Remember I said that packaged curricula are written by school people and so reflect an institutional approach. One of the manifestations of this is the fact that the materials are designed for children to progress through them at the same steady pace. One book may, for instance, call for a page of work to be completed per day. But what if your child finishes a page of math, thinks it's fun, and wants to go on to the next page? (There really are such children, honest.) Is there any reason he shouldn't be allowed to do so?

No. Not if he's learning at home. If he were in school, it could be a problem because there would be a schedule demanding that he close his math book and attack the next subject. Besides that, if all the children in the class were allowed to proceed at their own pace, they could all conceivably be working on different pages at the same time. This would mean the teacher would have to explain each step in the work to each child individually instead of taking a step at a time with the whole class. It would make a tremendous increase in the workload and the time involved.

This is a good illustration of the difference between mass instruction and individual instruction. The individualized arrangement at home allows a student to satisfy his curiosity by plunging ahead of the schedule in the curriculum guide. Some students finish two or even three years' worth of math (or another subject) in this way, and if they wish to do so they should be so encouraged. Remember how demotivating it was in school to have to close your book on a fascinating subject and switch to something else?

One of our sons took a course in high school economics that would have taken a full year in school. He worked through the book in a month simply because the subject came easily to him and he put in some extra time. We think he learned the subject better at the accelerated pace because there was better continuity. When he read the last chapter it had only been a month, rather than nine months, since he had read the first.

    The principle applies the other way as well. It may be that the curriculum guide calls for a faster pace in a given subject than your child is ready for. So, ignore the curriculum guide. Children aren't all the same, even if schools assume they are. Respect the seasons of your child's life and if the season hasn't come when he is mentally or emotionally ready for something in the curriculum schedule, change the schedule to meet the needs of your child. Don't try to change your child to suit the schedule.

    By the way, pace does not necessarily reflect success. If your child is ahead of schedule in one subject and behind in something else, don't assume it means he's "good" in one subject and *slow* in the other. Children learn in spurts, not at a steady pace, and the spurts come at different times in different subjects. Also, studies show that earlier isn't always better (see Raymond Moore's book, *Better Late Than Early*). According to the research, children do better in some subjects by starting earlier than usual and in other subjects by starting later than usual.

    It seems that our minds, like our bodies, develop at uneven rates. Certain skills may be hard for a certain child to learn at age eight but come to him quite readily at age ten. Personally, I wouldn't be at all concerned if you didn't start *required* academics with your child at all before age ten or eleven, because I have seen enough to know that he could easily complete in five years the learning we usually spread out over twelve. The reason that it's normally spread out is, I believe, threefold: 1.) The usual method of teaching en masse rather than individually, making everything more cumbersome; 2.) It makes jobs for more teachers; and 3.) We start too many things too early, thus causing for some children problems that take more time to work through than if we had waited for full readiness.

One day in the grocery store Marilyn and I ran into a friend who was a first-year home educator. When we asked how it was going, she replied that her fourth grade daughter was having trouble learning division. She had done well with multiplication, so she had the facts well in hand, but she just couldn't seem to make the transition from multiplication to using the same facts in division. That wasn't too surprising, because while multiplication and division use the same facts (2x2=4, 4/2=2, etc.), the two processes are vastly different. We asked our friend a few questions and finally suggested that she wait six months and then try division again. She did so, and her daughter picked it up without a hitch. Somehow, her mental growth just hadn't been ready for division at first.

Well and good, you say, but how do I know whether my child really isn't ready for something or if he's just being lazy? Good question. The answer is that if he's not lazy in other things, he's probably not being lazy about the problem subject. For instance, if Johnny mopes and drags his feet when told to wash the dishes, you should think twice before accepting his excuse that some disagreeable academic subject is just too hard for him. On the other hand, if he's responsible in tackling unexciting household chores and plows ahead through his other studies, he probably really is having trouble. Confer with your spouse about it, get opinions from some other sensible people, and if you can't find a way to get him over the hump leave him alone for a while. He may need more time for

Chapter 4 **Curriculum**

intellectual development or it may be that just a rest from the stress will do the trick.

Teach the head through the hands

Hands-on learning projects are especially important in the early years. They make learning more enjoyable, they provide some variety to balance the book work, and they help to illustrate for the child the usefulness of knowledge, the natural connection between learning and doing.

For example, if you're studying weather in the science book this month, have the children check the outdoor thermometer several times a day and make a chart showing the temperature at sunrise, noon, and sunset each day. Buy a rain gauge and chart the monthly rainfall the same way. Do an experiment with steam to show how clouds are formed.

If you're reading about ants, buy an inexpensive ant farm and the children can watch the ants operate from day to day. If you're studying fish, buy some new and unusual ones for the aquarium. If you're learning map skills, let the children make some maps—of the house, their bedroom, the United States or whatever. It really helps them pay attention.

You can find plenty of learning projects in books in the public library. Or, if you simply must spend money, you can order our booklet, *Fun Projects For Hands-On Character Building* from the materials list in the back of this book.

By the way, one of the indicators of a good textbook for younger students is the number and quality of hands-on projects and experiments included. For example, see the fourth, fifth, and sixth grade science books from A Beka book publishers.

A Few Words of Caution

There are a few typical glitches to which home educators fall prey, especially in their first year or two. Some of these little caveats may seem a bit repetitive after what you've read thus far, but they represent stumbles and fumbles that aren't uncommon, so I think they're worth mentioning.

You can't use it all

If you're just starting to educate at home, no doubt you're excited. But don't let that get the better of you when you start cruising the book fairs. If you go out and spend a thousand dollars on books and materials I assure you you'll never use all of it. I know it's bewildering to behold, walking the aisles between book tables in the display area of a state convention or flipping through glossy pages of a colorful catalog. But you just don't need a lot of stuff. And so much wonderful learning is available free through the resources of your church, the goings-on in the community, that set of encyclopedias for which you paid a fortune but that you never use, and the local library.

Don't get too fancy

Along the same line, don't be beguiled by the products that present themselves as high tech or state of the art. Learning is an old art, and it hasn't really changed that much. These days, everybody is excited about computers. Computers are wonderful, but I don't believe they'll ever replace books, for example, the thesaurus. A thesaurus is a book of synonyms. To avoid using the same word too often in writing, I often go to my thesaurus for a synonym. I now have a computer with a thesaurus function, but I prefer my book. Why? Because in the process of flipping through the pages I see hundreds of words that are unfamiliar to me, and I often indulge in the pleasant distraction of stopping on my way to my target word and learn the meaning of a new word by the synonyms listed for it. The same applies to a dictionary, an encyclopedia and the card catalog at the library. The computer takes you on a straighter course to your target but you miss rubbing shoulders with a lot of exciting new knowledge en route.

Another example of the high-tech sales pitch is the hype given to some of the new math systems. I'm only acquainted with one or two of them, and I'm sure some are quite good. But I know in a couple of instances the reason the program seems so *advanced* is that it pushes algebraic concepts at little children who have not yet had time to master their basic math, which for most people is more important. If the program, whether it be a computer program, a math system, or a *new* method of reading instruction, looks complicated or appears to overemphasize its cutting-edge newness as a sales ploy, beware. Don't invest your money until you're comfortable that you know what's going on.

Start where they are

Especially if your children have been in school and you're taking them out to teach them at home, there may be some confusion as to where to start out with their work in each subject. Don't accept the school's assessment of your child's ability. Every year that system labels millions of bright kids "learning disabled" while cheerfully handing diplomas to thousands of graduates who can't read them.

Let's say you have a son who was in sixth grade at school. You plan to start teaching him at home this year and so buy the materials intended for seventh grade. You may find out, however, that Johnny isn't "in seventh grade" in every subject. He may rip through the science book and tell you he learned all that stuff two years ago. Or he may look at his first math assignment and instantly go cross-eyed with confusion. You have to start somewhere, so if you don't know exactly where Johnny is in every subject, start by having him try the subjects as they are given in the curriculum intended for his age. If some subjects are old hat to him, order the books for the next two or three grades up and turn him loose. If another subject seems to be throwing him a curve ball, back up until you find the point at which he is competent and move ahead at a pace he can manage. There is no shame in working through material his younger brother is doing at the same time. The shame is in him doing less than his best because you failed to recognize where he was and go from there.

Stay the course

There is plenty of room to experiment with curriculum, but it can be overdone. We have a friend who has switched programs entirely several times over a period of years. You can lose a lot of ground that way as the children (not to mention their mother) have to get used to a different setup. Some people seem compelled to make

Chapter 4 **Curriculum**

these changes whenever a new curriculum package comes along with attractive wrapping and clever advertising. Maybe it's a manifestation of the yuppie syndrome—gotta have the latest thing. Beware of fads in education.

We have another friend who is always talking about switching curricula because her children don't seem to be performing up to their ability. We, however, know enough about the material she's using to know that it's good stuff. Her problem isn't the material, it's the teacher. She isn't educating her kids in an orderly and diligent way. She allows too many things to distract her and so wastes valuable time and energy.

There's no reason you can't make some changes in your curriculum from time to time, but beware the temptations to do so for no good reason. Usually a major change entails a setback, so be sure you're gaining an advantage that offsets the disadvantage.

K.I.S.S.

Remember that little saying? I remember hearing it tossed around among the members of my high school debate team: Keep it simple, stupid. It's good advice as a rule of thumb for home educators.

The *it* to which I refer is your general approach to home education. Learning, although it involves incredibly complex happenings beneath the surface, is at living level a simple thing. Sure, I know the American way is to channel kids through a huge monstrosity of a system that burns billions of dollars yearly, employs thousands of specialists with litanies of college degrees behind their names, and speaks its own language of extraterrestrial-sounding terms that no outsider understands. But don't forget that this societal edifice of ours has failed to produce literate adults anywhere nearly as well as colonial schools were doing at the time of our nation's birth. A lot of the complexity of the system is created by design for the purpose of keeping the general public off balance and in awe of the mighty and mysterious *School System.*

New hypotheses and fashions are constantly slithering out of the swamps of imagination to sprout wings and go swooping through the swirling winds of mass educational theory. New psychological pathologies are discovered regularly to explain why poor learning originates in design flaws of the children or the maladies of the social environment rather than any failure of the *System.* Fresh discoveries and state-of-the-art techniques promise to revolutionize the science of education, and usher in a utopian age in which everybody will learn to unlock the ultimate intelligence within each of us.

But forty percent of the adult males in the city of Boston can't read.

I have so much more confidence in you, the parent, than all the experts the government school system can offer. In fact, if you're new at this I probably have a lot more confidence in you than you have in yourself. It is, after all, a little intimidating to hear strange terminology and strange theories bandied about by others who seem to know just about everything there is that's worth knowing.

Pick up a home education magazine or the program for a state convention and you'll see words and phrases permeated with clinical flavor. Dyslexia. Attention Deficit Disorder. Right brain/Left brain. Multisensory. Learning Disability. Interactive. Some of it makes sense when put into layman's terms, and some of it is hogwash start to finish. The thing you need to remember is that good learning was going on for centuries before all these highbrow terms were ever heard. As John Gatto has said, professional interest is best served by making that which is easy to do seem hard. Hence we have inscrutable terminology for common-sense ideas and vague, enigmatic concepts alike. Professional jargon, you know. Very impressive. Nobody wants to argue when you can throw around terms like that.

Don't be intimidated. A lot of it is smoke and mirrors, a sales pitch for snake oil. The fact is that average parents all over the country are producing home-educated children who far outstrip their moms and dads academically. A good recipe for education is two parents, one or more children, and a pile of good books. The same principles that make one successful in any arena, work in learning as well: diligence, motivation, planning, resourcefulness, and good judgment. I'm not saying that there is no value whatever in any of the concepts represented by professional terminology. I'm just saying that people were learning, happily and productively, before education became the realm of the professional. Has it ever occurred to you that Abraham Lincoln made it from the log cabin to the White House without ever knowing that he had a right and left brain?

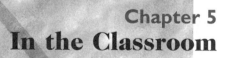

Chapter 5
In the Classroom

NOW FOR THE NITTY-GRITTY. How do we organize our structured teaching time to implement the principles we've been talking about? I suppose no two families operate their *classrooms* exactly the same way and I think that's as it should be. Just bear in mind as you read this chapter that I'm suggesting general principles and telling how we do it. I'm not saying that you should do it precisely as we do, just using our experience to illustrate the application of the principles.

Classroom Procedures
Be there

It's very important that the teaching parent (or in some cases, the older sibling) be physically in the classroom when the bookwork is going on. Some parents seek out curriculum packages that allow the student to be almost entirely self-directed. I suspect this is mostly because Mom wants to be free from the classroom so she can be working on some of her many other responsibilities. But Mom's attention is a great motivator and is especially critical to certain types of learners, as we will see later in the chapter.

Marilyn's method is to assign the day's work in a subject, get the preschoolers started on a project to keep them occupied, then check back with the older children to assess progress. The time lapse between giving the assignment and checking back may be only a few minutes or considerably longer. Some children need less supervision than others. Marilyn checks back more frequently if she is introducing a new concept that day, to make sure that if anyone is having trouble they won't repeat their mistakes long before she detects the problem. When the day's work on a given subject is completed, she goes over it and corrects it, explaining to the child where improvements are in order and giving encouragement when it's needed.

Control the schedule

Control your schedule, but don't be so rigid that the schedule controls you. There are extremes to be avoided in both directions. Don't be too tight. For instance, if a science project is going really well and the whole family is breathlessly watching an egg hatch or a mixture of chemicals turn funny colors, don't drag everybody away because you're two minutes late starting on math. But don't be too loose. Even if you have to rearrange the schedule occasionally and once in a while take a whole day off, beware lest you communicate that "school" is an optional part of the schedule. It's possible to grow so lax that you start hearing children say, "Aw, Mom, we've been working hard. Let's skip school today!" The regular classroom time must be a given.

Talk about what's happening

You can save your children a lot of boring writing if you'll keep abreast of what they're reading and otherwise working on. If you can satisfy yourself that they are paying attention and learning, you can dispense with most of the written evaluations the textbooks offer in the form of questions to be answered in writing. Especially for younger children, for whom writing is hard work, answering your questions orally will be much more interesting and they will have more energy to apply to learning instead of reporting.

Keep the little darlings occupied

A scene that has lingered for years in Marilyn's mind is of our little Laura, then about two years old, sitting in the middle of the dining room table while her siblings studied all around her, pulling the felt-tip markers out of their holder, popping the caps off, and throwing them in all directions. Laura had a way of doing such cute little tricks with so much glee that we've at times had to just stop what we were doing and laugh. But we've found that our household routine can stand only so much of that sort of diversion. So in order to get anything done, especially by way of learning, we've had to plan just as carefully to keep the preschool children occupied as to teach the older ones. Because little children always want to feel that they are doing what the older people are doing, they feel dreadfully neglected if they can't *do school* when the other children are doing it. They aren't hard to please. Just supply them with some paper, paste, round-pointed scissors, crayons, and coloring books and they will usually stay happy. Having gotten the babies out of your hair, the challenge is to keep the paste out of theirs.

Use older siblings as teachers

I can't remember now which book it was, but I remember reading John Holt once where he told about an experiment in which sixth graders with reading problems were assigned to teach first graders to read. The results were fascinating. Not only did the sixth graders improve their reading skills by working with the younger children, but the first graders learned to read better than other first graders who were taught by the teachers. Needless to say, that project was not repeated, but it serves to illustrate the fact that children can teach children. This can multiply Mom for all practical purposes, and is valuable training in childrearing for the older kids. I suspect it also builds self worth in the younger children when their older siblings are willing to be so closely involved with them.

Sprinkle the bookwork routine
with a seasoning of special things

Books are wonderful, but variety is wonderful, too. Besides, books have limitations that can be supplemented by special projects and events. Art projects, science experiments, guest speakers, field trips, and the like can spice up your routine. Be creative.

Use drilling as a stepping stone

Personally, I don't like rote memory work any better than anybody else. Still, some of it is necessary. We must memorize letters and blend sounds to learn to read, and we must learn the math facts to move ahead with math. But some parents and some curriculum writers overdo it. Phonics is a good example. We use a lot of material from a supplier who loves phonics, as they should. But they make sure that everybody gets enough phonetical instruction by shoving the phonics to the student all the way up into the third grade. We don't do that. The reason for phonics is to teach reading. When our children learn to read well, we drop the phonics.

Make spiritual training
a regular part of the instruction

You may be able to find a Bible curriculum that you like to add to your regular program. In addition to that, you need to work with your children on specific aspects of Christian character. At the risk of bragging a little, I think rather highly of my wife's projects in our book, *Fun Projects for Hands-On Character Building.* These character-building ideas originated with Marilyn's method of turning problems into projects, and identifying character needs through conflicts in the family and applying Scripture to them. There are a number of good character-building books on the market. Among the best of them is the *Character Sketches* series by Bill Gothard, available from Institute in Basic Life Principles in Oak Brook, Illinois. Recent years have seen the publication of quite a variety of new books for children, including some well-illustrated ones teaching specific character qualities or Biblical doctrines. Go shopping. It's fun.

The Four Motivational Types

We're not talking here about the learning styles; visual learner, auditory learner, etc. You'll learn by experience how each of your children learns most effectively. Some thrive on hearing, some thrive on the printed word, others are driven to dive in and get their hands on things. You will learn to recognize those natural tendencies and cooperate with them by watching your children at their learning over time.

What we want to cover here are not the categories of method, but of motivation. Marilyn has noticed four distinct motivational categories among our children in the classroom. She has had to adapt to the special needs of each type of child and it's been enough of a challenge that she thought it might be helpful to share them here.

She does not say that any of your children will fit one of these types perfectly; not all of ours do. But I think you'll find it helpful as you recognize some of these categorized traits in your children, to have access to some of the techniques Marilyn has developed in meeting the needs of hers.

#1: The self-directed learner

This child likes to set his own goals and thinks in terms of challenging himself. He loves to pick a target and shoot at it. He is bored with too much guidance and needs to work at his own pace. Not easily discouraged by setbacks, he seems to do best when allowed as much freedom as possible to design his own plan, set his own pace, and set his own objectives on his way to the ultimate goal.

#2: The sensitive learner

The sensitive learner has a tender heart that won't take a lot of adversity before growing melancholy and discouraged. You need to stay close to him, supplying him with achievable goals and lots of verbal praise and encouragement to keep him from bogging down in the tough spots. The sensitive student usually does a good job in the end because he tends to think in terms of perfection. But that same perfectionist tendency can discourage him because he so often feels that he doesn't measure up to his own standards. It also sometimes causes him to work slowly and painstakingly. He should not be rushed unnecessarily, as he may tend to feel that he has been pushed into finishing the work for a deadline at the expense of satisfying his heart that it was done right. Frequent hugs are good medicine.

#3: The slothful learner

This student is easily distracted from a mundane task because he's not overly excited about sustained effort to begin with. He doesn't push himself but can stand some pushing from without to go beyond doing the minimum required. He needs plenty of attention and some accountability, as he is more likely to skim through an assignment just to be able to report it done than to stop and think what the reason for the assignment might be. He needs to be shown the rewards of persistent effort because his automatic tendency is to reason that it is unwise to put anything off until tomorrow that can be put off until next year. Sticks and carrots are most useful with this child, but don't forget to love him even though he tweaks your patience at times.

#4: The steady learner

The steady learner is a consistent fellow who generally leams fairly easily in most subjects, although like anyone else, he finds some subjects more interesting than others. He tends to move through material steadily, without spurts or sputters of motivation. He tends to get a lot done because he is not easily distracted, discouraged, or defeated. He's an overall good student, and little trouble to teach.

About Subject Areas

I'm sure by now you've gathered that we don't see education as consisting of only that which is learned on weekday mornings in structured lessons. There is learning going on every hour human beings are awake, and it happens in many different ways. But if you're a parent you already know that. You've watched your children learn about housekeeping, home maintenance, personal hygiene, human relations, bicycle riding, and a million other affairs of daily living. But there are those things that are usually best learned through books and by means of a planned and organized system. To complete this chapter we'll share a little about how we handle each of what most of us call the *school* subjects.

Reading

We are absolutely committed to phonetical reading instruction. It is the only method of formal reading instruction that makes any sense and has been demonstrated to work. Before starting phonics, though (around five or six years of age usually), we lay the groundwork for reading by reading to the children. Of course that's not the only reason we read to our kids. We do it because they love it, because we enjoy it, because it is good for our relationship, and because they learn from the material we read. It also demonstrates to children the wealth of information and pleasure that can be found in books. It is being read to that furnishes most children with their motivation to learn to read.

That desire to read usually comes before the child is ready for phonetical instruction. Our children often have several of their little books memorized so they can sit and *read* them to their younger siblings before they even begin to learn phonetical sounds. When we do start teaching them vowel and consonant sounds, using the flash cards, etc., we usually don't go more than about fifteen minutes with it per day. That has been sufficient for our children and more than that seems to be boring.

By the way, some children learn to read without phonetical instruction at all. Our son Rickey cracked the code at age four just by watching the letters in his little books as we read to him, associating the words with the pictures and asking what sounds were made by certain letters he pointed out. Most of our children have taken phonetical instruction and we don't know how many if any of them would eventually have learned to read as Rickey did—because they didn't want to wait, they wanted to learn to read right now.

It should be remembered that the purpose of phonics is to teach children to read. Once they have cracked the code and are reading comfortably on their own, we drop the phonics. Phonics teaches the child only the sound of words, not their meaning. So it is important to pronunciation but not to comprehension. We use mostly A Beka materials to teach phonics, and their program calls for phonetical instruction to continue up into the third grade. That has never been necessary for any of our children so we've always dropped the phonics before then, and usually before they complete the first grade materials in their other subjects. I suppose the reason A Beka takes phonics instruction so far is that their books are written for school use and they want to make sure everybody *gets it.* Being able to dispense with the parts of a curriculum that our particular children don't need is one reason we don't send our children to school. There is a better use for their time than teaching them something they already know.

Once our children have learned to read, they have all loved to read. If your children don't, toss out the television. That's usually the problem. As for reading comprehension and vocabulary, that comes mainly with time. Seeing words in the context created by other words is the key to a large vocabulary and the skill of discerning meaning in reading material. Keep plenty of good books in the house and occasionally *plant* a new one on a bed, on the coffee table, or in some other conspicuous spot and often it will be picked up and perused out of curiosity even though the topic or the cover may not have interested the child enough to seek the book out on his own.

Writing

We teach writing to our children in a pretty typical way, using workbooks with traceable letters. We don't rush writing; we generally let the children begin to learn to read first so that the effort of learning to write makes more sense to them. As they pick up writing skills, they always want to use them to write to Grandma or whomever, and that is an excellent exercise because it usually gets them an answer back, which is great motivation to write more.

We have found that children will correct a lot of writing mistakes on their own if left alone for a while, so we're not quick to jump on them if they don't make letters perfectly. This may be difficult for you if you're a perfectionist type, but it's important. You don't like to be criticized for things that don't really matter, and things that will eventually be automatically corrected don't really matter. Besides, it is much harder for six-year-old children to trace and reproduce symbols on paper than for an adult. A small child's motor skills are undeveloped as yet, and writing, which seems so natural to us adults, is work for him. Don't be hard on him.

John Holt points out that a small child learning his letters sees them not as symbols for sounds but as pictures of objects. Why? Because every time a child makes an intentional shape on paper with a crayon, it represents the shape of something he has seen and is trying to reproduce (I say intentional shape, because children will often just scribble to see what sort of marks appear on the paper). For instance, if a child draws a stick figure of a dog, it is a dog to him regardless of which direction it is facing. If he turns the paper upside down so that the dog appears to be lying on his back, it is still a dog.

When the time comes that we begin to teach the child to make letters, unless he has begun to learn to read or has been read to enough to understand that letters aren't pictures but symbols that stand for sounds he may not understand that the letter can be backwards. In fact he still may not understand it at first. To illustrate this to yourself, draw a stick picture of a simple chair from a side view. You can do it with three lines. If you draw the same chair facing the opposite way, it's still a chair. Now try to explain to a tiny child that a small *b* turned backward is not a *b* but a *d*. If the child doesn't yet see the relation between symbols and sounds, he won't understand. Even if he is reading some, he still may find writing laborious and his letters to Grandma are so much work that he can't be bothered with which side of the "stick" the circle is on to make a *d*. Fortunately, God has gifted grandmothers with supernatural powers of discernment, and when informed in writing that little Johnny loves the stuffed "boggie" she gave him for Christmas, Grandma understands. Reversal or other imperfections of letters will usually be cleared up by the child on his own, but if not, wait until you're sure he is old enough before you make a major point of his mistakes.

People need lots of practice in writing to do it neatly and communicate effectively in writing. But most parents and teachers make the mistake of requiring a lot of pointless practice writing. By pointless writing, I mean writing that is done not for the purpose of communicating, but exclusively for practice. There are too many useful opportunities for writing to subject children to the boredom of writing practice sentences, lists of spelling words, vocabulary words, or whatever. Those exercises must have originated in torture chambers. If your child isn't doing enough writing of his own volition, then don't assign writing as if it were punishment, but rather give him a list of friends or relatives who would love to receive letters from him and who would write back. Older children can write letters to the editor, politicians, etc. I list some of those projects elsewhere in this book, but no doubt you can come up with any number of worthwhile projects on your own.

English

We don't start teaching English until third grade, although the publisher whose English book we use does produce texts for first and second grade. We have found that the things taught in the first two grades are usually learned automatically and with less effort through reading. For example, the curriculum would require the student to write out a whole sentence just for the purpose of having him capitalize the first letter and place a period or question mark at the end. Our children have all learned to do that in the natural course of reading, so we don't waste their time with the pointless writing. If you feel the punctuation practice is needed in your child's case, you might want to bypass the writing part by using typewriter correction fluid to white out the punctuation marks on a few pages of an interesting story, make a photocopy of it, and give it to the child to insert the punctuation. When he is finished you can give him a copy of the original text and let him check his work against it, marking his mistakes with red ink. If a reward would be helpful, this project would lend itself well to that, as you could count the punctuation marks you whited out and give the child a raisin, candy, or coin for each mark he inserted correctly.

From the third grade up we generally follow the course laid out in the textbooks. As in any other subject,we use the book as we see fit, omitting exercises we believe are unnecessary for the individual child, assigning extra work in some areas if it seems needed and always looking for useful projects to replace pointless exercises where practice is required.

Math

We use a mathematics program that calls for fifteen to twenty problems per day. We formerly used a program that called for forty practice problems daily. But we have found that our children haven't needed that much practice to move ahead with the program, so Marilyn usually circles about ten problems of those given for the day and has the children work those. If one of them needs more practice than that, there are plenty more practice exercises where the others came from. For the beginners,

Chapter 5 **In the Classroom**

we have fun workbooks and also assign little learning projects in which they count beads, raisins, etc. and do simple exercises in adding and subtracting with those objects.

History

We teach history in a pretty typical way, with a series of good textbooks. We use Christian books because the secular ones all leave out the work of God in world and American history. We let the children read through the material at their own pace, supplementing the texts with books we buy and check out from the library. We find the writings of the people involved in making history, such as the diary of Franklin or the memoirs of Robert E. Lee (actually compiled by his son) very enlightening. Living in Virginia gives us the advantage of being within driving distance of many historical places, including Appomattox, which is only thirty minutes from our home. We also have time lines, posters of the Presidents, history games and puzzles, etc. See our booklet *Creative Learning Projects* for other ideas.

Science

Science is the only subject in which Marilyn really uses unit studies. If the unit topic for this month is Rocks and Minerals, the children all read the section about rocks and minerals in the science text for their grade. Then they collaborate on projects, experiments, or a field trip if appropriate. There are lots of interesting books in the library on different aspects of science and a number of science magazines for children, but watch out for evolutionist underpinnings and political correctness.

Spelling

We have not taught spelling to most of our children. They seem to become good spellers as they become good readers: by reading a lot. One of our boys had a little trouble, so Marilyn worked on it with him for a couple of months and that was sufficient. Most good readers are good spellers because they see the words over and over, and they pay attention to what they read. There are exceptions, though. I suspect you will usually find, as we did with our son, that if your child is doing great in reading but poorly in spelling, he's probably just weak on a couple of the spelling rules. For instance, if he doesn't understand "*i before e except after c*" he could misspell several words (believe, receive, retrieve, deceive, grieve, etc.), but be violating only the one rule.

Marilyn suggests that you don't bother with spelling until the fourth grade, in order to give the child plenty of time to learn what he can from his reading, and then demonstrate the rules, if any, on which he needs work.

Art

There are art textbooks available through a number of publishers, as well as art workbooks for younger children. In addition, you may want some of your children to take lessons in one form of art or another. Some craft stores offer lessons in various craft skills, and you can usually locate art lessons through word of mouth or newspaper ads. Marilyn now lets Katie teach the younger children art one day per week.

Music

Music appreciation courses can be ordered that include cassette tapes of music for study. We are providing piano lessons for all our children. Not because we expect all of them to continue indefinitely but because we feel it is a good basic exposure to music theory that will help them to sample the musical world. We also found it helpful to have an autoharp in our home because little children can easily learn to make decent music with it, it can be used for accompaniment when singing together as a family, and it is a good introduction to chords. At the time we bought ours they sold for just over a hundred dollars, but I expect they are considerably higher now. If you invest in a few used musical instruments to have in your home, one or more of your children may find a lifelong interest by just experimenting with one.

Geography

We use a standard Christian geography text with our children. We like it quite well, but we have found some creative ways to supplement our teaching that add so much more to geography. We have made salt-and-flour relief maps of the U.S. and the world, and globes of balloons covered with papier-mâché and painted with oceans and continents. Speaking of globes, Marilyn found one in the form of an inflated kickball that actually lasted a year or two under the punishment such toys receive around our house. She also located some geography sheets for children's beds with pictures of oceans, continents, and the animals that live on the respective continents. Ours are worn out now, but it used to be common to walk into Matt's bedroom and find him on his upper bunk teaching one or more of his little sisters the names of continents from his sheets and pillowcase.

Beyond the Basics

As our children have moved into the teen years we've introduced more specialization. In our family the kids generally finish what we consider the equivalent of a high school education around age fifteen. By that time we work with them in government, economics, typing, and consumer math; the practical things that will help them function in the adult world. At the same time we try to make provision for them to pursue their areas of special interest. Because politics is an interest shared by all our older children, we subscribe to some conservative political magazines, encourage them to read appropriate books, and help them with their involvement in campaigns and other political business. Because of our unusual family situation our older boys have not had as much freedom for exploring different areas of learning as I would have liked. For years I had to have their help in the family business, which occupied a considerable amount of their time. Now the LORD is granting us more freedom, so we're eagerly awaiting future developments. Our eldest son has just accepted his first paying political position and that will no doubt be interesting. But all children are different, so no doubt they'll soon be educating us about other career fields as well. I look forward to exploring with them.

A Word About Testing

As you may have discerned, Marilyn and I don't lose a
lot of sleep about testing. The real test of childhood
education is adult life. But tests are of concern to most
parents because so many other people (including
prospective employers) judge us by test scores and, of
course, there are often testing requirements written into
state laws regulating home education. Marilyn's suggestion
is that you don't worry about testing all year, but just
the last two weeks before the test. In the first place, skip
the year-end testing unless it's absolutely required by law.
In our state a portfolio of the student's work can be
submitted in lieu of test scores. If you do elect to take
the test, prepare your children for it not by cramming data,
but by making them familiar with the test forms to be used.
If they are the computerized blacken-the-oval answer
sheets, emphasize to the children that they need to check
carefully on each question to make sure they haven't
skipped one. If they fill in the answer to question twenty-
four in the line intended for the answer to question twenty-
three, then their entire answer form from that point on
is going to be skewed and their score is in big trouble.
Marilyn says that on one of the major national achievement
tests, the spelling test for younger children consists of
circling the misspelled word in a list of five. That might be
a helpful practice exercise for preparation week.

　　　　We don't test our children because we feel
no need for it. But if you want your children to do well
on achievement tests in the spring it would be a good idea
to give them tests from time to time just to acclimate them
to the mechanics of taking tests. However, I wouldn't advise

that unless you are sure you can do so without creating test anxiety in them. If I tested my children, I'd treat each test as just another learning exercise and not as an evaluation of their learning at all. I would want them to see periodic tests as just practice runs and not get all excited about the year-end test, either. I wouldn't even discuss their scores with them. I don't want my children to come to regard tests as the vindication of their learning. Tests have come to wield a lot of influence these days. Marilyn and I are well satisfied that they have some value as tools of assessment, but because it is our children we're teaching, we feel that we can evaluate their progress in other ways. Besides, tests have limitations even in terms of the present. They certainly can't be trusted as prognosticators of long-term success. Harvest time is the test for the farmer; adult life and service are the test for my children.

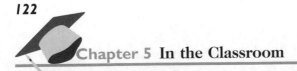

> *A good recipe for education is: two parents, one or more children, and a pile of good books.*
>
> —RICK BOYER

Chapter 6
Making Learning Fun

I LOVE THOMAS EDISON. Edison, to me, is the epitome of what home education is all about. He went to school at the age of seven and stayed for a total of three months. He was a bright, curious boy and his constant questions were a challenge, if not an outright annoyance, to most adults. It was this inquisitiveness, in fact, that ended his school attendance and began his education. One day little Thomas heard the schoolmaster tell the district school inspector that the Edison boy was "addled." He went home and told his mother, who promptly went to the school to give the teacher a piece of her mind (of which he evidently had a shortage) and withdrew Thomas from enrollment. From that time on, his home was his classroom.

Mrs. Edison had the unusual notion that learning could be fun. She made a game of teaching her son, preferring to call it *exploring* the exciting world of knowledge. Curious Thomas was delighted at this and within a few years, he had so blossomed as an explorer that his mother could no longer keep up with his questions. When she bought him a chemistry book written by a famous educator, he determined to try every experiment in the book to see if he could find mistakes in the author's statements. He collected over a hundred bottles for his chemicals and developed his own laboratory.

At the age of twelve Alva, as he was called, took a full-time job selling newspapers and snacks on a train. In his spare time he experimented with chemicals in the baggage car. He even printed a newspaper, the *Weekly Herald*, the first newspaper to be published on a moving train. At sixteen he was hired by a Canadian railroad as a telegrapher, at which time he created his first invention—

a device to make the required hourly telegraph report to Toronto even if he, the operator, was asleep. He came close to being fired when his boss, who didn't seem to appreciate creativity, found him snoozing on the job.

Edison's commercial inventing career started at age twenty-one with an electric vote-counting machine that he patented and tried to sell to Congress. They wouldn't buy it because it interfered with their practice of trading votes during the forty-five minutes required to take the roll call. This may have been a fateful happening in the young man's career, because he was so frustrated at having invested effort in a creation that wasn't wanted that he swore that ever after he would devote himself to the "desperate needs of the world."

The rest, as they say in the books, is history. Besides the invention of the light bulb and the phonograph, Edison invented a multitude of devices ranging from his vote counter to a method of making synthetic rubber from goldenrod plants. Between his own inventions and the improvements he made on the innovations of others, Edison patented more than 1,100 inventions over a period of sixty years. Henry Ford suggested that the period of Edison's life should be referred to as *The Age of Edison*, because of all the contributions the inventor had made to mankind. A friend of mine expressed similar admiration: "Why, if it wasn't for Thomas Edison, we'd all be sittin' around watching TV in the dark!" Proof that Edison earned the respect of those at both ends of the intelligence scale.

Thomas Edison was arguably the greatest inventor of all time. Because of his success, I think it's valuable to ask ourselves what it was that made him so brilliant. It certainly wasn't "higher education," because his institutional career was only three months long. I'm willing to assume that part of his success was due to natural talent, because others have evidenced unusual talent in art, music, athletics and other fields. But surely his upbringing had a part in his long and useful career as well.

After taking him out of school, Mrs. Edison made her front porch the family's first classroom. Her style of teaching was quite different from the local school, where children were punished for asking too many questions. She posed questions for her son and herself to discuss together, and took time to help Alva search for answers to his own questions. Rather than burdening him with hours of bookwork, she taught him the basics and provided time and materials for him to experiment on his own. He was only twelve when he took a full-time job but his curiosity continued to drive him to learn, as it had not been stunted by endless hours of confinement in a schoolroom. Throughout the rest of Edison's life, his mother's conviction that learning should be fun stayed with him and made him first a great learner and then a great leader.

Happier Learning, Better Learning

I believe that a desire to learn is an integral part of human nature. I once asked a friend, whom I consider quite brilliant, how he had learned so much about technical and mechanical things. He gave me a simple formula: Curiosity plus exposure equals learning. That sounds so basic that it almost seems too easy. Yet that principle is really at the bottom of most of our learning success. Edison was curious,

and his mother provided for him to get exposure to the things in which he was interested. So, he learned.

Both sides of the same coin have been experienced by millions of people throughout history. Some, like Edison, have access to the experiences that enable them to pursue their interests. They become knowledgeable as they seek to satisfy their curiosity. Others may have the same interests, but no exposure to what's happening in those areas of interest, and so they never learn as much as they could have learned. Still others, and perhaps most of us, never know how many different aspects of our world could have been interesting to us if only we had been exposed enough to find out.

When I was a teenager, an uncle of mine who was a career police officer told my mother that I should go into the practice of law. He based this opinion on his observation that I could talk my way out of anything. Well, I was pretty evasive. Mom thought it was a great idea because she knew that law is a lucrative and respected profession. But my impression of a lawyer was a guy in a white shirt and necktie (I still hate ties) who shuffled papers in a fancy office and carried on arguments in unintelligible words. It just didn't sound interesting to me. On the other hand, my best friend was the son of a lawyer and knew that part of the job was standing up for the rights of people who couldn't defend themselves. That would have appealed to me had I understood it, but somehow I didn't. A few years later my friend and I were in our early twenties, he was a lawyer and I was painting houses. What a sad thing is wasted talent. And no, I don't mean that he would have made a great house painter.

Years ago when I was just beginning to study the field of education, I had an interesting conversation with a lady who was a veteran fifth-grade teacher. She wondered out loud why it was that at age five children were so curious that adults couldn't answer their questions as fast as they could ask them, yet when they reached the fifth grade five years later, "We practically have to knock holes in their heads to be able to get anything in there!"

At the time I hadn't developed a strong opinion, but I did have a gut feeling that it had to do with locking active little kids into desks and cramming them full of stuff that seemed to have been designed for boredom value. In the dozen or so years that have elapsed since our conversation, I've been able to identify a number of elements that contribute to the failure of children to learn as well as they should. I've found that removing children from the dulling atmosphere of school solves some of the problems, but not not necessarily all. Some home educated children are failing to learn much better than they did before being taken out of school.

We parents and teachers talk a lot about motivation, as if children were automatically uninterested in learning and had to be artificially induced to do it. In fact, humans are naturally curious and skillful learners. This is evident very early in life. Put a baby of crawling age down on the floor and roll an orange past him. Chances are he will, unless distracted by some other interesting object, examine that orange in a very intelligent way. Likely, he will apply all five senses to the orange. Seeing it, he will crawl after it and catch it, then look it over. He will quickly learn to recognize its size, shape and action (rolling) visually. He will touch it and learn something about its

Chapter 6 **Making Learning Fun**

texture, its weight, and how much force it takes to make it roll some more. He may bang it on the floor and hear that it is rather quiet, say, as opposed to one of his toy trucks being banged on the hardwood. If he picks it up and tries to put it in his mouth (very likely), then he will learn that the peel has a pleasant smell when bitten but tastes too tangy and burns his lips. Thus he has applied seeing, hearing, smelling, tasting, and touching in just seconds or a minute or two.

Oranges, car keys or Christmas tree ornaments, it's hard to find an object that is not interesting to a child of that age. So if you stop and think about it, the problem with young children is not making them want to learn, but channeling their curiosity without discouraging it until they are old enough to learn the boundaries of propriety. But something happens between crawler stage and fifth grade that stunts this natural desire to learn. Few children at ten years of age still have the urge for broad exploration that they displayed as toddlers. What goes wrong?

There's not room here to take the negative tack and discuss all the counterproductive elements of institutional schooling; besides, it has already been done by people much more capable than I. John Holt's excellent book, *How Children Fail*, is the best work I've read on the subject. But to address the issue from the home educator's point of view, in this chapter I'd like to offer some suggestions that Marilyn and I believe can help learning happen by putting some of the natural satisfaction back into the process.

Develop a Learning Lifestyle

We need to drastically expand our vision of home education. Most of us start with the idea of simply doing at home what is usually done in schools—an adult assigns work from a curriculum package and helps the children to whatever extent is necessary. That's fine for starters. It's pretty non-threatening and so encourages timid parents to have a go. But we need to move on from there to broaden our vision of learning until it includes the things we learn outside the assigned bookwork, twenty-four hours a day, for a lifetime. And that means the parents, too, are learners. Our children need to see us learning in order to understand the importance of learning.

To apply our discipleship model of home education, we need as parents to build a lifestyle of service-oriented learning and involve our children in it with us. Sometimes we use *structured teaching* times that bear a lot of similarity to school. But that is only one color in the rainbow. We also use *guided exploration*, as when a child is interested in music and we provide instruments, recordings, books and paid lessons, though we can't teach music ourselves (that is, *I* can't). Field trips also could be considered guided exploration, as could a trip to the library to research a particular subject. It would be a form of guided exploration to invite an interesting person to dinner for the sake of giving our children the benefit of his knowledge and experience.

I don't know that it's a critical distinction, but children also learn effectively through what I call *free exploration*. This differs from guided exploration in that the child not only initiates it by expressing an interest, but pursues the subject in his own way without a lot of guidance from his parents. My eldest son's political interest would fit in this category. He became interested in politics by reading history and hearing Marilyn and me talk about the presidential campaign of 1980. Soon he was reading the newspaper (at six or seven years old) and before long he was receiving political magazines. He was working as a campaign volunteer before he was old enough to drive to headquarters. Elected his party's county chairman at nineteen, he long ago surpassed his parents in knowledge of politics and government. Nearly all this learning resulted from his own free exploration.

Much of what we learn comes through this method. The reason it works so well is that it is built upon the child's original interest, so the motivation is ample from the start and no pumping up or reinforcement is needed. Also, interest and aptitude often travel in tandem, so motivation and talent combine to produce excellence. Free exploration was the channel for the curiosity of Edison and Franklin, and proved to be the seedbed of genius.

It's been fun to watch this work in our own family. Besides being the politically uneducated parents of a politically astute son, Marilyn and I also have sons who show considerable mechanical ability, a daughter who is a self-taught author, and an eleven-year-old son who can shame his parents in world geography. All these (and the same things you see happening in your children) are the fruit of simply allowing children the freedom to pursue their interests. I suspect that we would have seen less of it had our kids been limited to the time and energy remaining after a seven-hour day of answering other people's questions in school.

Another channel of learning is what I call *incidental learning*. That occurs whenever we gain new knowledge that doesn't result from an intentional effort to learn. For example, I learned that people in Brazil speak Portuguese. I had always assumed that everyone in South America spoke Spanish, but I met a new co-worker who was Brazilian and he set me straight. The information came as a surprise to me so that I remarked on it to my family that evening at supper. My ten-year-old spoke up:

"Oh, yeah, Dad. Brazil is the only Portuguese-speaking country in South America."

I was taken aback. "And just where did you get that bit of information, Dr. Einstein?" I asked.

"Oh, I read it somewhere."

He had learned it incidentally, too.

There is a negative side to developing a lifestyle that encourages good learning. The idiot box will have to go, or at least be used under stringent guidelines, such as no one who is under thirty years of age may watch it. Oh no, you groan. Here he goes again. But if that's your reaction maybe you need to consider the reason that it so threatens you for me to say it. Sorry, but television is killing our society. It's the assassin of the American intellect and the enemy of a learning lifestyle.

Read Marie Winn's excellent book, *The Plug-In Drug*. It's probably available at your public library and should be required reading in every Christian home with a television. Winn quotes studies showing that the very act of watching television reduces creativity. This is true regardless of what type of program is on. The body releases chemicals during television viewing that act as a mild depressant and cause the brain to operate at less than

Chapter 6 **Making Learning Fun**

its normal capacity. This mind-numbing, sedative effect is what makes so many parents depend on television as a babysitter. Children not only limit their physical movement while watching the tube, but get so mesmerized that they sit quiet as well as still. More spiritual parents may use videos in place of regular programming, but the effect is much the same. Children become addicted to the cheap and unchallenging entertainment of the glowing blue tube, and parents become addicted to the electronic nanny. I don't say you shouldn't have a TV in your home under any circumstances. But I do say that you shouldn't own one if you don't control it properly. And very few families do.

Along with television, take inventory of the other things in your home that may be counterproductive to learning. Shallow or seedy music should be pitched ruthlessly. Comic books are junk food in the literary diet. A lot of the toys circulating today are garbage. What would the old time martyrs think of Mutant Ninja Turtles?

Even if your children are already addicted to brain- stunting entertainments, don't let them stay that way. Throw out the junk immediately and spare not for their howling. And as you pitch the garbage, replace it with good stuff. One of the reasons children spend so much of their time in front of the television is that they haven't learned how many interesting things there are to do elsewhere. Make frequent trips to the library and bring home lots of good books. If the children don't show much creativity in selecting a variety of books, take the initiative to check out several that you select yourself and leave them lying around where somebody will idly pick one up and leaf through it sometime. We call this *planting* a book, and it works to expose children to things they wouldn't seek out on their own. And of course there's nothing wrong with required reading.

Healthy toys such as kites and bicycles are good for outdoor play, and when inclination or weather dictate indoor activity, there are Lincoln Logs, Tinker Toys, checkers, and a great variety of educational toys. Ask your librarian for a book or magazine on the subject, as they are harder to find than uneducational toys. Invest a few bucks in astronomy equipment, lab sets, anatomy models, etc. In other words, clean house and replace the harmful pastimes with healthy pastimes. It's fun.

Besides organizing your surroundings to promote learning, organize your schedule with the same goal in mind. This means involving your children in the responsibilities of the home to the extent of their ability. Some children waste time on questionable entertainments because they have too much time to be entertained. This is bad because of the junk they're ingesting, but also because of what they are missing by not being active in the business of real living. Children who spend their time helping care for younger siblings, working in the family business, keeping house, doing home repairs, cultivating gardens, participating in the family ministry and accompanying their parents as Mom and Dad pursue their own interests, are children who are on the road to fulfilled adulthood.

Involve the Whole Child

The human senses are like windows. The more windows we open, the more fresh air we allow into the house. The more we make use of all the child's senses, the more learning we let into his life.

The senses were designed to work together. This is one of the problems with mass education: we separate children from the real world, in which all their senses can be active in taking in and assimilating information, and lock them into age-graded cells in which the atmosphere is about as far from the real world as you can get.

A child can read a book about firefighting, for instance, and learn a certain amount of useful information. But there are ways to go much farther than that. I once had opportunity to watch some firefighters at work extinguishing a small blaze in a suburb not far from our home. I struck up a conversation with a boy of about fourteen who had ridden over on his bicycle for the occasion. He turned out to be a fire buff who was fascinated with firefighting and never missed an opportunity to watch the action. As we talked I noticed he was carrying a portable scanner. He told me that he kept it on as much of the time as practicable and responded to the scene whenever a fire occurred within cycling distance of his home. No doubt he had read books about firefighting, but they couldn't supply the noise of the sirens and the water flying in hissing streams from the hoses. Nor could books convey the sting of acrid smoke in the nostrils, the adrenaline rush of battling an inferno, the courage and commitment of the firemen sweating inside their protective clothing. It takes input through channels other than the eyes trained on a printed page to give the full picture.

If you want to teach your child about erosion, let him read about it in his science book. But do more than that. Take him outside in a rainstorm and let him see erosion happening. Stand under an umbrella with him in the middle of your garden and watch the muddy torrents cutting gouges in the dirt and carrying all that precious compost you shoveled last summer, right across the yard and over into your neighbor's garden. He'll see the runoff, smell the wet earth, feel the mud pulling at his boots and hear the thunder, wind and rain, along with your moaning over your lost labor. Maybe you'll even be inspired to bring him back in dry weather and experiment with cover crops or mulching for erosion control. It would be very educational. And it sure beats doing all that shoveling over again.

The more senses are involved in a learning activity, the more stimuli are admitted to the brain and the more retention takes place. This is why we need to involve the whole child as much as possible. When we shackle the body, we shackle the mind.

Use the Child's Individual Interests

Like my young friend with the scanner, every child has one or more interests that particularly motivate him. Finding creative ways to use these interests as springboards into related subjects is a worthwhile challenge for the teaching parent.

For an example, let's say ten-year-old Suzy is interested in horses. When she was a toddler she loved coloring books full of horse pictures. Now she wants riding lessons as a Christmas gift; has a bedroom full of horse posters, calendars, and figurines; and is beginning to hint that perhaps the family should sell the house in the suburbs and move to a ranch in Montana. How can you use Suzy's interest in horses to stimulate her interest in other subjects?

Geography

Assign Suzy to find out what geography has to do with the development of different horse breeds. For instance, Arabian horses were bred by Bedouins in the deserts of northern Africa for their stamina and smooth gait because of the harsh dryness of the region and the long distances that must be traveled. Appaloosas were developed by the Nez Perce Indians of the American West because of the need for sure-footed horses in the their Rocky Mountain homeland. Expand on that and look into the geographic origins of other breeds.

Mathematics

Create some horsey math problems. For instance, Clydesdales are large horses, adults weighing from 1,500 to 2,000 pounds. What is the average weight of an adult Clydesdale? Or, the United States has about _ 3,000,000 horses. About five percent of these are draft horses rather than saddle horses. How many draft horses are there in the United States? Comparisons of numbers of different breeds, or horse populations at different times in the nation's history, could be used for studying graphs, etc.

Science

A cross between a horse and a donkey is called a mule. Why can't a mule be mated with another mule to produce a baby mule? (They're sterile.) How are the different breeds of horses developed? What is the difference between the way a horse digests its food and the way a cow does?

The possibilities are endless. Learn to cultivate your creativity and your child will learn to do the same.

Make Use of Wise Timing

Timing involves at what age a child learns a given piece information and how he learns it. Readiness is one of the first considerations. Is your child mature enough for the discipline of phonics just because he is six years old? Most children are, but some aren't. Don't assume that your child is ready to learn to read at six just because that's what your curriculum guide calls for. On the other hand, if your four-year-old wants to be read to constantly and is ceaselessly asking you what this or that letter says, don't hesitate to start him on phonics and see if he can move ahead with it just because it's not indicated by the curriculum guide. Children are people and people are different.

Another aspect of timing is the length of time spent on subject matter. I learned in dog school that if training sessions are too long, the dog will lose motivation and just go through the exercises half-heartedly. If the sessions were too short, the dog wouldn't learn as much as he should in a day or week of training. With children it's a little more tricky because they may learn that if they fuss a little, Mom will conclude that they're just not up to doing bookwork today and let them off. Children are not only more intelligent than dogs; they are less honest as well. But time and experience will demonstrate what the real needs and tolerances of your children are.

The thing to keep in mind is that interest can be stifled either by too much or too little time given to the task at hand. You can keep it up until the child is sick of it. On the other hand, you can interrupt a child in the middle of something just because your paper calls for it, and thus frustrate him when he's halfway through reading a selection, writing a poem, or working out a page of math problems. Again, you will learn the patterns of your individual children with observation and the passing of time.

Make Wise Use of Rewards

There are some things we need to learn that just can't be made enjoyable in and of themselves. For me, arithmetic facts would fall in this category. When you run into one of these roadblocks, rewards may be the technique you need.

Don't be afraid of the concept of rewards. There is a difference between a reward and a bribe; that being that a reward is offered to induce us to do right and a bribe is offered to induce us to do wrong. The world is full of rewards and they are just as legitimate as punishments. We see rewards used for motivation in the workplace, the home and elsewhere, so there is no reason they shouldn't be used occasionally.

When Marilyn runs into a task that the child must conquer but which is terribly onerous to him, she will dream up a reward system. In the case of my beloved math facts, it might involve getting a stated reward for memorizing a certain number of math facts and being able to recite them in five minutes. Rewards can be quite simple and still be effective, especially for younger children. The value of the reward to the child should reflect the difficulty of the assignment given. One thing we have used as rewards for our children is tropical fish. We have several aquariums and the children all enjoy getting different kinds of fish and watching their behavior through the glass. There's a built-in control system that prevents overpopulation, too. The fish are very cooperative in that they keep dying off as fast as the children can earn rewards.

Connect Learning with Needs and Purposes

It's not very motivating to put out a lot of effort on a project that has no important purpose and meets no evident need. This is where so much of schooling misses out. So many of the things done in schools are done in a milieu detached from the world outside. Children do exercises for no purpose they can see, other than to be evaluated on how well they did them. They do reports to be read only by people who already know more about the subject than they themselves know. They write letters that the theoretical recipient will never read. They do math problems just for practice, knowing full well that if they make a mistake the consequence will be abstract, as in a point marked off, rather than practical, as in running out of chicken feed and having to make a special trip to town before the week is out. This dissociation of the skill from the natural use of the skill removes much of the meaning and motivation from learning.

If you want your child to learn to write persuasive letters, don't assign him to write to an imaginary person on an hypothetical problem; let him write to the editor on a real need in the nation or the community. If you want him to learn map skills, assign him to help you plan the route for your next vacation. If you want him to learn the relationship between the capacities of measuring cups, enlist his help in cooking.

It doesn't take all that much ingenuity to come up with more motivating and useful assignments than writing a report on what you did last summer for a person who cares not the slightest whit what you did last summer.

Be Involved Personally with the Child

The core of discipleship is the relationship between the master and the disciple. The essence of home education is the relationship between the parent and the child. This is why we don't like workbook-oriented curricula or video home-education programs. They tend to prevent communication rather than enhance it.

As in the dog-training scenario, relationship is the key. You can do more to motivate or de-motivate your child through your relationship than with any material rewards or punishment. Children have a natural desire and need to please their parents. If we show them that it is in fact possible to please us and how to do it, they will exert considerable effort to do so. If we park them in front of a video screen we neither motivate them by our relationship nor improve the relationship.

My tendency is to notice the little things that are wrong instead of the big things that are right. An employee of mine once told another manager, "Rick doesn't want it done right. He wants it done perfect." There was something to that, I'm afraid. So I try to be careful to notice and comment on the positives in my children, and not speak too quickly when I see a negative. A lot of the negatives will disappear as the children grow older and discover on their own what makes their way smoother and what doesn't.

Marilyn has learned that she has to stay in the classroom during the hours her children are in the textbooks. If she doesn't, things go haywire. One day she assigned the children their lessons, then walked into the living room and sat down with her notebook to do some planning. A couple of minutes later one of the children came into the room with her school book and sat down on the couch opposite Marilyn. A minute or two later, here came another child and within five or ten minutes they had all drifted into the room with Mom. None of them had spoken a word to her, and most had their eyes glued to the page of the book as they walked. But there is a certain gravitational pull to a mother that attracts her children like tacks to a magnet. We would be wise to work with this natural attraction and use it as a motivator.

It works for fathers, too. Once when my son Tim was small, I asked him if he'd like to do a little job for me. What kind of job, he wanted to know. I said, "Oh, for instance, how would you like to paint the mailbox?"

"Ehhhhhhh…"

"How about rearranging the silverware drawer?"

"Ehhhhhhh…"

"How about planting the new rose bushes?"

"Ehhhhhhh…"

Chapter 6 **Making Learning Fun**

"Tell you what. How about if you pick one of these jobs and you and I do it together, just you and me?"

"YEAH!!!"

The glory of sons are their fathers.

Stay close to your children as they work. They need the security of your nearness and the encouragement of your interest. Nothing can take the place of your personal involvement.

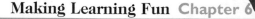

Part 3

Other Things

Chapter 7
Spiritual Training

The advantage I have in writing this chapter is that I know I have a sympathetic audience. Every responsible Christian parent wants to train his or her children to serve the LORD. Another advantage I have is that most parents don't think they're doing a very good job of that at present so I can rest assured that I have your close attention.

One chapter is by no means enough space to cover the subject adequately, but I'd like to at least illustrate the place of spiritual learning in home education, lay down some Biblical principles for doing it, and give a few practical suggestions as to how it can be done.

Why is Spiritual Training Important to Home Education?

Parents seem to sense instinctively that their children's spiritual needs are critically important. When we present the Learning Parent home-education seminar, the session on Hands-On Character Building is usually the most enthusiastically received hour of the seminar. Maybe part of the reason is that Marilyn usually presents that session and she's much easier to look at than I am. But mostly I think it's because moms and dads (and especially moms, who seem to be more spiritually sensitive than us dads) have as their heart's desire that their children develop Christlike character, and hunger for practical methods of cultivating that.

Chapter 7 **Spiritual Training**

Educational priorities

Parents are right in feeling that spiritual training is central to all learning.

> **MATTHEW 6:33** *But seek ye first the kingdom of God, and His righteousness; and all these things shall be added unto you.* KJV

One of the characteristic mistakes of novice home educators is to spend so much time and energy on academics that there is little left for the spiritual things. Compounding the pressure of curriculum goals and legal testing requirements is the fact that really good spiritual training materials aren't as readily available as math and history books. It takes more work and creativity to address the spiritual issues adequately.

But you must persist. We have found through many years of teaching at home that when we seek spiritual things first, academics come along satisfactorily. When you get into the later grades especially, your children will be learning about politics, current events, economics, social issues, etc., all of which are addressed from the Godless point of view in a million written and electronic channels. They need to have developed by then a solidly Biblical worldview that will help them see through all the babble.

Mind conditioning

Programming Scripture into the minds of your children is the best way to prepare them to learn. Two plus two equals four, and there's a reason that's true. It's true because God says so. He is the author of truth and the creator of the universe with all its order and consistency.

When we learn truth, whether mathematic, scientific, historical or whatever, we are learning more about the nature of God.

> ROMANS 1:20 *For the invisible things of Him from the creation of the world are clearly seen, being understood by the things that are made, **even** His eternal power and Godhead; so that they are without excuse.* KJV (emphasis mine)

The "they" in that verse refers back to verse 18, which talks about ungodly men who suppress the truth in unrighteousness. My understanding of the intent here is that man knows as much about God as he chooses to know. Even those who have never seen a Bible are responsible to God for as much of Him as can be seen in His creation. So the process of discerning and understanding truth about the universe depends on our spiritual conditioning. If we are spiritually receptive, true academic information finds fertile ground in us. If not, we are subject to becoming very confused about the world around us.

Our trusty old example, evolution, perhaps epitomizes this. The theory of evolution is just that, a theory. It can't be confirmed by empirical evidence. Yet it's taught not as theory but as fact in most schools. Why has it taken such firm root in our academic structure? Because the higher-ups in the educational system choose to believe it. At the same time, they choose not to believe in creation, which takes less faith to believe. Creation, after all, requires only that I believe in the existence of something beyond my power to understand: the formation of something out of nothing by the power of an intelligent Creator. Evolution is more demanding. It requires me to

Chapter 7 Spiritual Training

believe in something that violates my power to understand: the creation of something out of nothing without the involvement of an intelligent Creator. The evolutionist's own laws of physics state that matter cannot be created or destroyed, but can only change forms. They also dictate that matter automatically goes from a state of order to disorder (as the process of decomposition), yet evolution requires matter to evolve from less organized forms (such as minerals or gasses) to more organized forms (such as tissues, organs, and organisms).

Why do people choose to believe a theory that requires them to deny their own reason? Because they are suppressing the truth in unrighteousness. They know by instinct that God exists and has certain requirements for their lives. Because they choose to be their own final authority ("...*ye shall be as gods*..." GENESIS 3:5 KJV), they subordinate their reason to their will and their foolish hearts grow darker (ROMANS 1:28).

What we want as Christian parents is the opposite of that process. So rather than starting with the assumption that God is irrelevant, we start with the assumption that God is basic to all truth about His creation. Because He has given us His Word as our textbook to the universe, that should be our foundational resource.

Our use of the Scriptures as text material goes farther than our reason. We certainly should approach it reasoningly, as when we look for references to a given subject. But we need to take the process beyond the information stage to the point that Biblical principle becomes our life philosophy. This is why the Bible so often mentions the process of meditation, as opposed to the process of study. Both are important of course, but meditation goes deeper into the spirit and character than study. Meditation should be seen as the internalizing or assimilation of Scripture, and reading, study, and memorization seen as steps in the process.

The mind that approaches every subject with the assumption that God's Word is true is moving in the right direction already. Still farther down the road is the heart that has been purified by bathing in the Scriptures. We have found that the more our children internalize Scripture, the better they learn anything. That makes sense. After all, life is a struggle between the flesh and the spirit. The spirit dominates when it is cultivated, so the struggle quiets down and there is less confusion and distraction. The sin nature, with its interest in the bad and disinterest in the good, is the one learning disability we can be sure is real.

How Do I Go About It?

As I said before, most Christian parents want to train their children spiritually but need some practical ideas on how to do it. My advice is to look around and borrow all the good ideas you can find. One man who was asked how he managed to be so creative in his ministry, answered that he defined creativity as forgetting where he borrowed the idea. Good thinking. Creativity is not just picking your own brain until your head caves in, but putting forth the effort to find and adapt the ideas of others to your own needs.

Chapter 7 **Spiritual Training**

Cleanse your home

The first step in ministering to your children spiritually is to clean the garbage out of their home environment. This would refer to any items associated with the occult—ouija boards, *Dungeons & Dragons*, books on witchcraft, etc. It would also include anything not obviously of an occultish nature but detrimental to spiritual growth. Among such influences would be most television programming, rock music, toys representing supernatural themes, etc. Light and darkness can't abide together, so make your home more suitable as a repository of light.

Saturate your home with Scripture

When our first child was born, we were quite young and very inexperienced in the Christian life. But my wife was very sharp and had a strong instinct for ministering to children. Having been a student teacher in high school and an education major during her one year of college, Marilyn was intensely interested in teaching her own children and when Rickey came along she couldn't wait to get started. He was still an infant when she began decorating the walls of his room with alphabet charts and other educational stimulators. Having little else to do with her time, my wife spent hours reading and talking to him in what I would have considered pretty one-sided conversations.   But within a few months we had moved to a different part of the country and come under some Biblical teaching that would revolutionize our lives. The result was that Marilyn stopped pushing infant academics at our son and started plastering the walls with Scripture. She found Bible story books for small children and began reading those to him, along with Scripture itself. She began to find all kinds of creative ways to build the Bible into the decor of our home. It was rather primitive in form then, as we were broke, along with most of our contemporaries. But she made construction paper and Magic Markers go a long way. We didn't know it then, but Marilyn had stumbled onto a Scriptural principle that is very important. Later we saw it expressed:

> DEUTERONOMY 6:6–9 *And these words, which I am commanding you today, shall be on your heart; and you shall teach them diligently to your sons and shall talk of them when you sit in your house and when you walk by the way and when you lie down and when you rise up. And you shall bind them as a sign on your hand and they shall be as frontals on your forehead. And you shall write them on the doorposts of your house and on your gates.* NASB

Without knowing it, Marilyn was practicing the principle of verse 9 when she started covering our walls with Scripture. Note that the verse talks about doorposts and gates. That refers to the physical structure of the home. That means God wants us to build the Scriptures into our visible surroundings as a constant reminder of Him.

Verse 8 says to bind God's words as signs on our hands and frontals on our foreheads. Frontals, or frontlets, were little leather boxes worn in Bible times on a headband during times of prayer. A verse of Scripture would be written on a slip of papyrus, rolled up and inserted into the box. The frontlet would swing with the movement of the person wearing it and bang him in the forehead. It was a physical reminder to honor God's law.

We were never really into headbands, but Marilyn did come up with a way to honor the principle of verse 8 by putting Scripture on other items of wearing apparel, such as T-shirts and sweatshirts.

As years went by Marilyn originated and collected tons of ideas for saturating our home with Scripture. When we began sharing her ideas for spiritual training projects in our seminar, we were deluged with requests to put them down in written form. So we wrote a homely little manual and later expanded it into a full-length book entitled *Fun Project for Hands-On Character Building*. It tells how to do scores of projects and gives information on where to get materials for them. But don't feel that you have to buy anybody's book in order to build Scripture into your home. We don't do anything that you couldn't come up with yourself. Many of our projects could be done by taking ideas from academic project books in the public library and adapting them to Scriptural material.

Note that verse 7 mentions four different times of the day when we are to communicate God's words to our children. They are when you sit in your house, when you walk by the way, when you lie down, and when you rise up. Evidently these are specific times of heightened spiritual sensitivity. Let's take a look at some ways in which we can honor the principles of the four times and the "doorposts and gates" concept.

When you sit in your house: this is usually mealtime, because it's about the only time of the day that all your children sit at once. Marilyn puts Scripture on tablecloths, plates and mugs. In our dining room she papered the walls and found a wallpaper border with

157

Spiritual Training Chapter 7

Scripture on it. The tablecloths can vary themes according to seasons of the year, Christian holidays, or the theme of any Scripture verse you care to use. She does this with fabric paints and also draws pictures to illustrate themes.

When you walk by the way: Most people don't walk from place to place much nowadays, but you can redeem some of the time in the car by singing or listening to Godly music, reciting Scripture memory verses, or playing car games like "Guess Who" in Scripture.

When you lie down and rise up: This refers of course, to bedtime and wakeup time. Here is where Marilyn really shines with her ideas. She plasters the kids' bedrooms with Scripture in the form of wall plaques, Bible story curtains, character-quality quilts, even wall decorations with Scriptural themes such as her stuffed Noah's Ark complete with animals and rainbow. She even went so far as to make macramé animals and give them Bible names. We have Caiaphas the cat, Jeremiah the giraffe, Enoch the elephant and others. One of her very best ideas was what I call the *Jesus and the Children* plaque. Maybe you've seen those neat art prints by Frances Hook in the Christian book store. One is a picture of Jesus surrounded by a group of little children and cupping the face of one child in his hands, in attentive eye-to-eye communication. It's a neat representation of the LORD's individual concern for children. Marilyn found a way to make it even better by cutting the child's face out and replacing it with one from a photo of one of our children. We hang this over the child's bed so that when he lies down and rises up he has a visual reminder of how special he is to Jesus.

Learn to use the book of PROVERBS

The Old Testament book of PROVERBS is a gold mine for parents. It contains more useful wisdom than one would learn in the process of acquiring ten PhD's. Being an exhorter, I especially love the book because it is so simple, usable, and practical. It could be called a textbook for parents because of its unique nature and its great value to parent and child alike.

The book's author is Solomon. He was the son of King David and took over the throne shortly before his father died. He was given special wisdom from God and riches and honor to go with it. The book of PROVERBS is an assortment of short, pithy sayings, some of which are original to Solomon, some of which were collected by him from the writings of others, and all of which are inspired by God as a part of Scripture.

Solomon was the wisest man in the world. The Bible says that men came from all over the world to hear him. In 1 KINGS 4:29–34 his learning is described as including music, biology, botany, and ichthyology. From other passages we learn that he was proficient in design, construction, government, finance, and just about anything else kings deal with. His authorship of PROVERBS, ECCLESIASTES and the SONG OF SOLOMON is evidence of his ability in philosophy and in literature.

So, how would you like to be able to teach your children the things that the wisest man in the world would teach his children? You can, by using the book of PROVERBS. PROVERBS was intended for Solomon's children, as evidenced by the fact that five of the 31 chapters begin with the words, "My son" and the phrase is repeated umpteen other times (approximately) throughout the book. It appears that the LORD specifically designed PROVERBS to tell us what to teach our children and what we should have learned from our parents.

We once categorized the entire book of PROVERBS by topics and we now offer it among our other materials. This is so that parents can have a list of verses in the book that apply to the particular subject they feel their children need to concentrate on at that time. There are about 50 topic categories and a given topic may be referred to by one or dozens of verses. Of course there is some overlap because some verses deal with more than one subject. This same project would make a great "school" assignment for your children.

Besides the topical study idea, there are several other ways to make use of the wisdom in PROVERBS. You can have the children memorize it, perhaps with a prize offered for each section or chapter conquered. You can read it into a tape recorder and make tapes for the children to listen to at naptime or bedtime (you might be surprised how much of it sticks with them). You can assign the reading of a chapter a day, connecting the number of the chapter to the day of the month. For example, if today is the tenth of the month, they would read PROVERBS chapter 10. If it's the twenty-second, they would read chapter 22. Because there are 31 chapters in the book, there is a chapter for each day even in the longer months. Another idea is to use PROVERBS for family devotions, reading and discussing the chapter that corresponds to the date. When you do this, learn to tell "example stories" about the text. My children got us started on this by asking me to explain what certain things in the daily chapter meant. For instance, they asked me about the shifty fellow in

PROVERBS 6:12–15 who winks with his eyes, signals with his feet and points with his fingers. I made up a simple story about two guys who conspired to rob someone by having one of them infiltrate the home as a handyman and then signal to his partner when the coast was clear for the heist. I was surprised how effective this little teaching tool was. It really grabs their interest and helps them understand.

It would be hard to overstate the value of this Old Testament book. It contains lots of good, important information and its simplicity makes it very usable. It really is a treasure chest for parents.

Introduce your children to Christian heroes

A great resource for parents is the abundance of Christian biographies available. One of the great inspirations and reproofs of my life has been my acquaintance with such greats as George Müller, Jonathan Edwards, Charles Finney, David Brainerd, Robert E. Lee, George Whitefield, John Wesley, and Hudson Taylor. The list could go on and on because there have been a tremendous number of Christian heroes who were biographized either in their own time or later. In the past few years we've noticed an upsurge in the number of Christian biographies written for children and young people.

A word of caution is in order. Modern biographies are written by modern writers and usually they are not of the caliber of the person about whom they are writing. It takes a great Christian to accurately pen a biography of a great Christian.

So buyer, beware and don't invest your money in just any biography on the shelf. Look through it first and be especially careful of those written specifically for children. There seems to be a lower quality standard in that arena.

With that one caution in mind, get out there and load up on good biographies. They are great in content because they teach the reader the spiritual lessons the hero was learning, and broaden the reader's vision and lift his sights. They remind us that it really is possible to do great things for God.

Good biographies make fun reading, too, because the lives of old-time Christians were often fraught with all kinds of adventure, danger, and strange experiences. Just compare that to some of the drivel masquerading as Christian children's literature today.

Fill your home with good spiritual materials

There are some great children's books available today besides biographies. Here again, selectivity is required because much of the production of these things is motivated more by financial profit than spiritual profit. But the good stuff is out there. We've found many good children's books on character and doctrine, and also some very good records and cassette tapes.

As for videos, the few I've seen are shallow, worldly and Scripturally inaccurate. With all the good books available, there is just no need to expose your child to the eye strain, addictiveness and mental numbing of the glowing blue screen.

And just as they did not see fit to acknowledge God any longer, God gave them over to a depraved mind...

—ROMANS 1:28 NASB

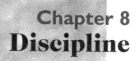

Chapter 8
Discipline

W**E'VE ALL HAD IT HAPPEN.** You get the kids all cleaned up and dressed in whole clothes, then pile them in the car and take them someplace. Into the restaurant or mall or church they go and before the outing is over one of them pitches a fit that measures 8.6 on the Richter scale. Everybody within about a hundred yards turns and stares, wondering why anyone would take such an obviously demented child to a public place rather than to the nearest exorcist.

Explanations are useless. Even if it's not inappropriate to stand up on a table and explain to the rapidly gathering crowd that Junior has an upset stomach, is coming down with chicken pox, got his eye gouged by somebody's elbow or had a bad dream while sleeping with his eyes open, nobody's going to hear you. They automatically assume your children are monsters.

The simple fact is that people notice children. And the effect is multiplied by the number of children you have with you. We used to get a lot of stares until our brood got so large that strangers assumed they couldn't all be in the same family.

So when you take your children out with you you're inviting attention. If you're sitting in your favorite restaurant and your five children are behaving themselves nicely, sooner or later some kind person will stop by on his or her way to the salad bar and say, "My, what well-behaved children. You don't often see children like this any more." You ladies will notice that this doesn't happen when you're out with just your husband. You don't see some sweet old grandma stop, pinch your husband on the cheek and say warmly, "My, what a lovely man you have here. Excellent saliva control, chews with his lips closed, no disgusting noises; you don't often see men like this any more," and then move on, leaving him with a final, fond pat on the head. No, it's kids who attract the eye.

That's one of the reasons, though by no means the only one, that it's important to have obedient children. The most obvious reason is to preserve the sanity of their parents. Beyond that, there are the reputations of the family, the church and the LORD Himself to think about. If you're a home educator, the public's impression of the movement as a whole will be affected by their impression of your children. But the most important reason a child needs to learn obedience is (no big surprise) that his own future depends on it. The attitudes inculcated in a child toward authority will powerfully influence his adult life in relation to his family, his work and the world around him. His effectiveness in serving the LORD will be determined by the presence or absence of an obedient heart.

Excuses, Excuses

One of the prevalent myths of our day is that teenagers are naturally rebellious. Even one well-respected Christian family psychologist has said that if his children were teenagers today, his goal would be just to help them survive adolescence. He seemed to be of the opinion that the pressures on teens are so great that survival to adulthood is about all we can hope for as their parents. Others say that young people are going to experiment with drugs, alcohol, sex, and whatever else is available during their teen years and that there is little or nothing that can be done to prevent it. The promise in PROVERBS 22:6 that children trained up in the way they should go will not depart from it, is usually rationalized to say that they will always return to the LORD eventually. Personally, I don't find much comfort in the thought that my children must all go through a prodigal period but will return to the LORD after burning their brains out with drugs and alcohol, or contracting AIDS.

Our society has become conditioned to accept teen rebellion. We have lowered our expectations of young people to the point where we don't seem to believe it's possible to have what people generally recognize as "good kids." But this doesn't line up with history or Scripture. The prevailing assumption among Christians that children will naturally rebel when they reach the teen years but return to the LORD eventually reflects the degree to which we have been conformed to the world in our attitude toward child training. PROVERBS 22:6 doesn't refer to returning to the LORD after a period of rebellion. It clearly talks about not departing.

This is not to say that children don't sin. Obviously they do. And there is a time in child development when they come to realize their parents aren't omniscient, that they can be wrong about things and they can be fooled. There is also a season in and around the teen years when they feel the urge to try their wings by making some of their own decisions. In the case of boys, I've come to the conclusion that there is some sort of a male dominance hormone that has to be managed during the growing up years as well. They seem to be more competitive and combative in their sports and games, as my many contusions will testify. There are some natural principles involved in the process of growing up that can result either

Chapter 8 **Discipline**

in responsible maturity or in sin, depending on how those natural principals are managed.

One thing that is not natural is peer dependency. This factor, especially in the teen years, is at the bottom of an awful lot of the rebellion we see in that age group. I think part of the reason for that is that the peer group makes children insecure about themselves because of the intense pressure for acceptance in the crowd. That insecurity then causes the young person to exhibit behaviors designed to get attention from others; bizarre dressing for example. It also adds to the temptation to rebel, as autonomy is one of the values stressed by the teen peer group.

Maybe it's never been easy to rear children. Certainly it isn't in our society now. But God gives us parents a responsibility to guide the young lives under our care into paths of responsibility and virtue. He hasn't written any exception clauses into the contract; He's just offered to give us babies in exchange for Godly young adults in the proper season. Like any other crop, they will only grow from seedlings to productive adult plants with careful, orderly cultivation.

The goal of child discipline is for our children to become adults with self-discipline. They will not always have their parents to control behavior, nor should they have. They will one day be parents themselves, with their own children to manage. Aside from the poetic justice of that (snicker, snicker), we parents should look forward to that time as a harvest season. It's not the fact that we have well-behaved four-year-olds that demonstrates the success of our efforts, but the competence of our children in training our grandchildren. Scripture says that grandchildren, not children, are the crown of old men (PROVERBS 17:6). Our grandchildren are the report card for our years of parenthood.

Building the Foundation

When the average person thinks of child discipline the thought that immediately comes to mind is of spanking. While that's a Biblical part of the picture, it is only a very small part. To think of spanking as discipline is like thinking of peanut butter as a complete diet. Peanut butter is wonderful stuff but it's only an element of a diet that, to serve its purpose, must contain many other elements.

The foundation of child discipline is a family lifestyle. A child is influenced not just by what happens to him, but what happens around him. The things that happen repeatedly, day after day and year after year, are powerful influences in forming his perceptions of how the world works. Bringing a new baby into a home where pandemonium reigns and spanking him when he takes his natural place as a part of the pandemonium is not a wise approach to the matter. In the following sections let's take a look at some of the important elements in a healthy discipline lifestyle.

Reverence for God

For human beings to live responsible lives, they need to have as a part of their outlook an inner assumption that the universe is a place of order; a system with a design and a Designer, which can be depended upon to give consistent results for given causes. The world in which we live is such a place, but the system is complicated on the surface and only faith can discern the simplicity at its base. Christians who are conversant with the Scriptures know that God supervises the happenings of the universe carefully and that His principles are universal. Whatever a man sows, that will he reap. We should want our children to understand this: that there is ultimate justice that can be deferred for a time but not escaped. Only as our children internalize this truth can we build real discipline in their lives. Discipline is not the behavior they exhibit when their parents are watching, but the behavior in which they engage when no one other than God is watching. It's entirely appropriate when confronting your child with a wrong you believe he has done but which you cannot prove, to remind him that while you can't be sure of what he has done, God knows what happened and why.

Discipleship mentality

Our children need to understand that our relationship with them is one in which we are training them to eventually be adults. In contrast with this is the common perception that normal child training is waiting for them to do something wrong and punishing them for it. While negative reinforcement is a part of the picture, it is what we do on the positive side of the ledger that sets the stage for effective correction.

Equally antithetical to discipleship is the notion of *sending* our children to be trained. In modern America, we *send* our children so much that we sometimes forget that our role is more to lead than to send. The idea of *discipling* a child is to take him, as it were, by the hand and lead him through life as we would through a strange neighborhood. But that's not the modern way. We send them to school to learn to read, write, count, and perform just about every other skill that usually comes through books. We send them to Sunday School and church programs to learn about God. We send them to all sorts of lessons and activities to learn to play music, sports, or other things of varying degrees of usefulness. By the time they are a few years old it becomes clear to them that the role of a parent is not to train them, but to send them to specialists to be trained. Their parents are functioning not as their leaders but as their dispatchers.

I don't mean to say that parents should teach their children everything they ever learn. Children grow in just a few years to a point at which their parents' knowledge can't begin to keep up with the growing ability and broadening interests of their sons and daughters. But in the early years there must be a relationship built in which the child understands that his parents are special people in his life; that God will direct his life through them. This will only happen if the parents and children spend plenty of time together, and the parents dominate the role of teacher for the first several years. The Scriptural way is for children to be parent-dependent while growing up, and deeply respectful and desirous of their counsel in adulthood.

> PROVERBS 23:22 *Hearken unto thy father that begat thee, and despise not thy mother when she is old.* KJV

Clear standards

You can't post a rule on your refrigerator door for every incident that can occur in a family. But your children can learn principles that will guide them in

Chapter 8 **Discipline**

discerning what is the will of their parents and ultimately, of the LORD. For instance, you could post a rule to the effect that children are not to grab toys out of one another's hands. But if you teach instead the principle of kindness, you kill more birds with one stone. That principle would apply not just to toy snatching but also to pinching one another or calling names. We want our children to learn not just prohibitions, but principles.

Respect for others is another principle of right behavior. It isn't respectful to interrupt while another is talking, or to rudely contradict what he has to say. If we can teach our children to think in principle, we will teach them at the same time a basis for behavior when faced with a situation for which they know of no established rule.

Underlying all rules and principles is the realization that some things are absolutely right and others are absolutely wrong. The Ten Commandments are not the Ten Options. We need to teach our children that what we are trying to inculcate in them is not just the best way of doing things to get the best results, but a heart of obedience to standards of character that are higher than human judgment and never change.

Example

One of the powerful motivators of child behavior is the example of others for whom they have respect. In the early years these others are for the most part parents and older siblings. If the behavior of these example persons is usually kind, responsible and selfless, then it will tend to engender the same behavior in younger family members. If our behavior is typified by selfishness, rudeness and anger, then we will reap the same in our children.

Here we have perhaps the greatest challenge in parenthood: modeling the character and behavior we want our children to emulate. But before you give up and decide you're just not cut out for parenthood, let me reassure you with a reminder that other parents aren't perfect either. If you lose your temper occasionally it doesn't mean that you have no authority to correct your children for throwing tantrums. What it does mean is that you're going to have to take responsibility for your attitudes and actions before your children if you want to have any credibility. When you blow your stack and offend a family member, you have the responsibility to quickly admit your sin and seek forgiveness. If you do that, then your family will see you growing and be encouraged by your example. In fact, I rather suspect it's quite a source of satisfaction to children to see adults have to admit that they, too, fail. But it all breaks down if a three-year-old pitches a fit and the parent spanks him in anger as a part of having a fit of his own.

Unconditional love

The balance for God's absolute standards of right and wrong is absolute acceptance. That means that while our children must know that there are certain things that they absolutely must or must not do, they must also know that their parents love and accept them no matter what they do. This is why punishment given in anger is more destructive than constructive. A spanking administered in anger may teach the child that he would be wise to avoid the offensive behavior, but it also teaches him that the parent's motive for punishing him is not to mold his character but to relieve parental frustration. That's a selfish motive and says to the child that his parents' love is conditional. Do certain things that please them and they will love you. Do certain other things and they will forget to love you.

Interdependence

I once knew a man of some means who had spent several years building a successful business and had finally reached one of his financial objectives by purchasing a nice house on a lake. One day I was out there with him and he was showing me around. It was quite impressive, with an attractive, rustic interior, sundecks, a nice boathouse, and a lovely view. As he gave me the tour I complimented him on his little weekend hideaway. He commented on how he had worked to get in a financial position to buy the place and the years and money he had spent in developing it with the extras.

"The ironic thing about it," he said, "is that now that I've got the place where I want it, I can't get my family together to come out and enjoy it."

He had been working so hard at building his business that he had neglected to cultivate his family life. Now his children had developed outside interests, his wife was involved in her career, and it was hard to get the family together for a weekend at the lake.

There are many pressures in family life, especially in those early years when usually there is a career or business to get off the ground. But if we allow ourselves to neglect building family unity until *later*, then we may find that *later* is too late.

When parents allow the family to drift into a pattern of every-man-for-himself living, it's only a matter of time until the emotional and spiritual commitment between members begins to wither. In the early stages the problem doesn't seem to be a problem at all. But the result of the process is that children grow up, go away to college, get married, move out of state for a good job, and start rearing children who seldom see their grandparents. The grand finale comes when Grandpa and Grandma find themselves stashed in a storage bin for retirees in Florida.

So what do mothball-scented grandparents have to do with child discipline? They serve as an illustration of what happens when family unity falls apart in the long term. We need to build in our children a sense of teamwork, of feeling important to the other family members. Little children need to have respect for parents and older siblings so that they appreciate how much there is to be learned from those sources. Their older brothers and sisters benefit from the responsibility of knowing that they are being watched with admiration and will be copied in their attitudes and behavior by those following behind them. We all need to internalize the lesson that no person is an island unto himself. Our behavior, right or wrong, has an impact on those around us.

These ideas are some of the elements in a foundation for child discipline. So much depends on the relationship between parents and child, and child and siblings, that we felt that this emphasis was necessary. The point to be remembered is that the teaching of heart obedience is a matter of lifestyle, not just cause-and-effect behavior modification techniques.

Training

One of the most helpful experiences of my life was the time
I spent as a student in dog school. That's what we called
the twelve-week course I went through as a young Air Force
security policeman in 1971. Having just completed six
weeks of basic training and five weeks of S.P. technical
school, I had elected to stay another three months at
Lackland Air Force Base in Texas (a vacation paradise with
which I was already quite disenchanted) to learn to train
and handle police dogs. Always an animal lover, I had been
deeply impressed by the "demo" the dog school students
had performed for us while still in S.P. tech. Their dogs
climbed ladders, vaulted over barriers, crawled through
pipes, jumped through flaming hoops, and attacked and
released on command. When they asked for volunteers to
go through the training and become dog handlers my hand
was the first one up.

Having that experience as a background, I began
to observe as a young man that most people's children
didn't behave nearly as well as our dogs. The reason seemed
obvious. Parents weren't training their children, but just
reacting to their misbehavior. And the corrections they
administered were pitifully ineffective. If they'd just given
me a leash, a choke chain, and five minutes with that child,
I could have had him jumping through hoops. My reasoning
was that children are smarter than dogs, so they should be
easily trained to behave at least as well.

Now that I'm a parent I've learned a few things.
For one, children really can be trained to be obedient. But
it's not quite as simple as I thought to make them that way.
Children really are smarter than dogs.

177

Anyway, I know now that a lot of things that I learned training dogs don't apply to children. But there were some lessons that have an application in the human realm. So, while I am not suggesting that you treat your children like dogs, here are some thoughts by way of illustration.

Relationship

Dogs and their handlers love each other. The first thing you do when taking on a new dog is to play with him and become friends. When you reach that point, he wants to please you and will bend over backwards to do so if you'll let him know how. Your dog must trust you. If you command him to climb a barrier and it falls over and hurts him, he'll hesitate to obey the next time he gets a similar command. You must never command him to do something he can't do, because you want him to believe that he can conquer any obstacle you give him.

Likewise with children. They want their parents to be pleased with them. Unlike dogs, they have a sin nature that keeps getting in the way with conflicting drives. That's one reason dogs are easier to train. But like dogs, your children must trust you. They need the assurance that if they give their best effort, you will praise them. They also need to know that your expectations are just; that you won't ask them to do more than they can do and then punish them for failing. Otherwise their spirits will be wounded, they will give up on pleasing you and concentrate on just doing the minimum required to keep you off their backs.

Instruction

Dogs want to please, but need to know what you want. Our dogs couldn't understand English (they were German Shepherds), so we had to teach them simple commands by demonstration. We would say, "Sit!" at the same time we pulled up on the leash and pushed down on the dog's rump. After about a trillion repetitions the dog would begin to associate the command with the action and know what he was supposed to do.

Children understand our language, so in that aspect they have an advantage over canines. But sometimes we parents still don't make our desires clear to them, either because we don't explain them thoroughly or because we're inconsistent in enforcement, sometimes correcting them for certain behavior and other times overlooking the same behavior. One of the most discouraging things we can do and one which I've caught myself doing, is to fail to let them know how they should act under certain conditions, then expressing disappointment with how they did act. Very discouraging to a child.

One of the most helpful projects we've ever done with our children is what we call Training Sessions. This is one of the projects listed in the Building Obedience section of our book, *Fun Projects for Hands-On Character Building*. One day several years ago, Marilyn came home from a shopping trip ready to tear her hair out because of the exploratory activities of our four little boys who, because of their age, couldn't be left at home alone. Later that evening, she and I sat down and talked the matter over. She said that the boys hadn't been intentionally disobedient; they were just normal, curious boys surrounded by bright colors and attractive packaging designed by experts to be appealing to the eye. It seemed that what they needed was a set of simple rules as to how to behave in a grocery store.

We made a list of a few things we wanted the boys to remember, such as looking with eyes rather than hands, staying in sight of Mommy, asking before touching, and using quiet voices. We explained the list to the boys and had them repeat the rules back to us. Then we took them on another shopping trip with Daddy along to remind them of the rules while Mommy shopped. It worked like a charm. The boys hadn't needed punishment. All they needed was a clear understanding of what was expected of them in a unique situation.

Praise

It's impossible to praise a dog too much for right behavior. In the case of a child it might be possible to overdo it, for instance making such a big deal out of a little deal that the praise communicates flattery, manipulation, or insincerity. But most of us parents are selfish enough that we tend the other way. We seem to think we're so wonderful that anything our children do to please us is no more than we deserved, so why spoil them with a lot of applause. Kids need to be told when they do well, and that requires extra effort. To tell them when they do wrong comes quite naturally.

We can take a lesson from Susannah Wesley on this. Her son, John wrote that when, as a child, he obeyed his mother's instructions, he was praised, and that the harder to obey the command was, the more praise she gave.

Correction

When I told my dog to sit and he failed to sit, I was supposed to correct him immediately and thoroughly. I was to jerk upward on his leash, slam down on his hindquarters with my other hand, and yell, "No! Sit!" at the top of my lungs. But correction had to be tempered with fairness. If there was a puddle where I had told him to sit, it would be cruel to correct him. It had been my failure in giving a faulty command.

With children it's critical to remember before administering correction that we had the first responsibility in giving clear instructions. If we correct a child for doing something he didn't know was wrong we will wound his spirit and damage our relationship. If it's a clear case of disobedience, the correction should be loving but thorough.

So there you have a few simple principles of dog child training from the most useful course of instruction I have ever been privileged to receive. The next time somebody asks what you've been doing lately, tell them you've been reading a book on education by a dog school graduate.

Dealing with Disobedience

Marilyn and I have found that there is a tremendous variation in the amount of negative reinforcement required by different children. We've had one child who would burst into tears at the sound of the word 'no,' another who wouldn't have been impressed had we pulled his fingernails out as punishment, and several degrees of response in between. One thing for sure: no child makes it from birth to adulthood without some chastisement, sometime.

Analyzing the offense

When it appears your child has disobeyed, the first thing to do is not pick up a switch and wear the bark off it, but rather to analyze the situation and see what's really going on. It's much better to let an offense go unpunished than to punish a child wrongfully and wound his spirit. You need to control your own spirit well enough to decide the issue objectively. If you aren't in condition to do that, you have no business administering correction at that time.

Did the child understand the instruction, rule, or principle he seems to have violated? You may have to quiz him a bit to see just how much he did or didn't understand.

Is his behavior a key to an unmet need? Don't get buried in pop psychology here, but beware of spanking a toddler who keeps getting out of bed if it's been an unusually hectic day and he has seen little of his parents. He may need a few minutes of Mom's or Dad's physical and undivided attention before being sent off to bed.

Did he do what was instructed but fail to do it immediately, cheerfully, and thoroughly? If so, he didn't obey.

For what offenses do you discipline? We suggest there are three categories: disobedience, disrespect, and irresponsibility. If you tell Junior to clean the aquarium and he refuses to do so, then he has disobeyed. If he does it but comments in a contemptuous voice that anybody can see it didn't need cleaning yet, then he is guilty of disrespect. If he has been told to clean the aquarium whenever it needs cleaning and it now has an inch of green algae floating on the water, then that's irresponsibility.

You may need to talk about the offense in order to clarify the issues. You might ask, What were my words to you about that? What did you do? Don't ever say, "Don't ever let me catch you doing that again!" Most likely he didn't intend to let you catch him this time.

Applying correction

If you have to spank your child, don't do it with your tongue. That only wounds the spirit and attacks the character. You want to communicate that you are punishing the behavior, not the character. Be careful to always let him know that while you absolutely disapprove of the behavior, you love and approve of him. A spanking hurts the backside, but a tongue cuts deep into the heart.

For that reason, you shouldn't ever spank in anger. I speak as much to myself here as to anybody else because it's awfully easy to fly off the handle with all the pressures of parenthood, and I've been guilty of it. But when we do, we have sinned against the child and should waste no time in asking forgiveness—not for the spanking, but for the anger.

When a spanking is necessary, use an inanimate object rather than your hand. I can't give you a scientific explanation as to why this is necessary, but the Bible always talks about the use of the *rod* in discipline. Hands are for patting, and for holding smaller hands. Wouldn't you feel terrible if you raised your hand suddenly and one of your children standing nearby flinched?

Use a rod that is appropriate for the age and size of the child. A light rubber spatula might be the tool for smacking a toddler's hand as he reaches for a forbidden object. An eighteen-inch oak ruler is good for larger children as it stings like mad but is too light to do real physical injury. I once knew a lady who used a light wooden spoon on a twelve-year-old boy who looked like a football player. Of course he howled and pleaded for mercy, but the performance was unconvincing to anybody besides his mother. On the other hand, a toddler must be handled much more gently.

The target of the rod is important. I've alluded to a smack on the paw for a little one who knows better than to reach for what he's reaching for. The usual target should be the buttocks, as this is the area of the body that best protects the child from injury. Be sure to protect the spine and kidneys with your free hand. Never, ever strike a child in the face. That endangers the eyes and, more importantly, wounds the spirit. I can't explain why, but I'm well satisfied that a slap in the face communicates rejection. Perhaps that is the significance of Jesus' admonition to turn the other cheek because it's a forgiving response to a deep insult. In any case, even dogs and horses resist having their faces touched except with great care.

Alternative corrections

Not every offense calls for spanking. There are a number of other ways to chastise and often one of them is more appropriate than corporal punishment. A child might be required to skip dessert or do extra chores, for instance. For older children and teenagers, there are the old standbys such as restriction of telephone time and driving privileges. I don't recommend restriction of television as punishment because most people shouldn't have a television in the first place. Restriction of TV is a reward, not a punishment. Reduction of viewing time makes the whole thing more attractive, which is about the last thing you want to do if you're wise. I also don't like the idea of using extra school work as a punishment because it tends to make academics seem onerous.

Restoration

When a child's offense involves a wrong not against moral law exclusively, such as in a case of slothfulness, but against another person, he needs to make appropriate restitution. It may be a simple appeal for forgiveness that's appropriate, or it may be a material sacrifice of some sort. For instance, if a child breaks a toy belonging to his sister through malice or carelessness, he should be required to pay for the toy or replace it. The principle of restitution is illustrated in some of the Old Testament criminal laws (see EXODUS 21:1-22:31), and is important in child discipline in order to fully restore relationships and teach responsibility for actions.

The Name of the Game

I've saved for last the most important issue in discipline. This is the spiritual side of the question.

> 1 SAMUEL **15:23** *For rebellion is as the sin of divination, and insubordination is as iniquity and idolatry ...* NASB

Remember that before sin ever came into the world it came into heaven when Satan and his angels rebelled against God. It was Satan who tempted Adam and Eve and he is behind all rebellion that has happened since. This is not to say that people don't have a will with which to choose right or wrong, it is just to say that there is more to child discipline than the control of outward behavior.

Personally, I tend to approach child training from a behaviorist point of view. Perhaps this is because my spiritual gift is exhortation, with its inclination to concentrate on cause-and-effect sequences. Or maybe it's because of my dog school education and experience in canine tutoring, which consists basically of behavior-modification techniques with no spiritual aspect to consider. But human beings are spiritual creatures and I'm learning that spiritual warfare is part of the discipline issue.

I've been slow to see this, but as my older children grow to adulthood and begin to spend more time outside our home and the presence of their parents, it comes to me with increasing clarity. There's a balance to be struck between diligent training on the one hand and spiritual effort on the other. We need to pray for God's protection over our children fervently and often, invoking the blood of Jesus and calling on God in His name to rebuke Satan and the evil principalities and powers.

We hope soon to produce an entire book on the subject of Biblical child discipline. We're finding we still have a lot to learn and there's a lot of important material in the Book that we haven't sifted yet. But to sum things up for our purposes here, I think we can say that the process of child discipline can be divided into four parts: lifestyle, training, correction, and spiritual warfare. We need to

Chapter 8 Discipline

arrange our lifestyle to encourage responsible, orderly behavior; spend time teaching our children through exhortation and character building projects; deal justly, lovingly and firmly with disobedience; and then commit it all to the LORD and pray fervently for our children.

Chapter 9
The Father's Role

BEING **DAD** to twelve children, I get a certain amount of credit I don't deserve. Many people seem to assume that because I'm father to a large family I must be good at it. That's not necessarily true, and I admit to being painfully aware of a number of character flaws. As a matter of fact, I've never been sure whether people are just kindly assuming the best about me or they admire my endurance. So, lest the reader waste the reader's admiration on the reader's humble servant (that means me), let me state at the outset that I have no illusion that size of family equates to quality of fathering.

Actually, if the number of one's progeny alone earned stars in one's crown, the world-champion dad would not be me or anybody else you know. That honor would without doubt fall to Baron, my neighbor's Irish Setter. Baron once fathered a litter of seventeen puppies. Born in my back yard. To my dog.

The qualifications for a successful father are unclear to more folks than just old Baron (who is no doubt still bragging) and in fact there seems to be some confusion even in the home-education movement. I've gotten the impression that the stereotype of a home-teaching dad takes one of two forms: He is either a classroom teacher who can't really be said to be educating his children if he's not in the books with them every morning, or else he's a housekeeper who helps out with the cleaning and laundry to free up more of Mom's time for teaching. I've never been comfortable with either of those two descriptions, so I went to the Scriptures and searched out some loopholes—er, guidelines that would shed light on the question.

We dads are at a disadvantage from the start. Women by and large, seem to come by much of their mothering ability genetically. I'll never forget how my wife responded when the present she received on her twentieth birthday was our first child. Every time the little one cried she seemed to know instinctively what the need was and was well on the way to dealing with it while I was still trying to find the OFF button. If my on-the-job-training experience is not decidedly atypical, then there is much bumbling done despite the best of intentions. It's a shame babies are too young too appreciate the advent of disposable diapers along with the disappearance of safety pins (a misnomer if ever I heard one) and the attendant bloodletting.

For those of us who have survived the complexities of early fatherhood, the home-education movement provides a new challenge. Nearly all of us in the movement were educated in the public schools, and consequently we seem to approach home education encumbered with a greater or lesser burden of assumptions that we picked up there. Because the picture in most of our minds is of a classroom with children in desks and one teacher (usually female) at the front, we're left without a clear job description for the home-school dad. Our understanding of the father's role is one aspect of the movement that still needs considerable refinement.

The problem is that we're using school as a model for education instead of going to Scripture and finding a Biblical pattern. Our concept of Dad as a teacher's aide derives from our false assumption that all or most learning takes place in a structured setting and that therefore to be involved in our children's education we have to be in the classroom between nine and noon every day. Likewise with the janitor idea. We assume that if we can't be a part of the structured teaching, then the best we can do is to grab the vacuum cleaner and allow Mom more time to work on it. But learning happens all the time. Whenever the father is with the children he is teaching them, actively or passively. And the answer to the increased workload of the home-teaching mom is not to add housekeeping to Dad's workday but to train the children to do what they are capable of doing in that line. They need those life skills for their own future responsibilities.

In our efforts to develop a useful seminar session on the topic of the father's role in home education my wife and I went to the Scriptures to find the Biblical functions God assigns to dads. Then we put our heads together, consulted with some other home-educators, and came up with some ways to apply those functions specificaly in the home-educating family. We found that the Bible has a lot to say about fatherhood. We were able to find seven specific functions of a father either by direct Bible references to human fatherhood or by using references to God in His role as our heavenly Father as a pattern for earthly dads.

Function #1: Provider

> MATTHEW 7:9–11 *Or what man is there of you, whom if his son ask bread, will he give him a stone? Or if he ask a fish, will he give him a serpent?* KJV

> 1 TIMOTHY 5:8 *But if any provide not for his own, and specially for those of his own house, he hath denied the faith, and is worse than an infidel.* KJV

The husband of a woman who teaches her children at home has a good deal to start with. In our part of the country at least, a couple can give their children a superior education for a year at approximately the cost of sending them to one of the local private schools for a month. With that in mind, Dad would be well advised to allow his wife some freedom in the use of the checkbook in supplying her classroom. My wife has earned my trust in handling money by making better use of it over the years than I could. Because she has the freedom to bargain hunt, Marilyn comes home regularly with some notable results. She buys in bulk when prices are low (e.g. school supplies in August) and watches for sales, especially those that aren't advertised. We don't have space here for a listing of her greatest triumphs, but one notable example was the time she found a store that had made an ordering mistake and was severely overstocked on boys' jeans. She came home with 50 pairs at a dollar a pair. Suffice it to say that she takes care of a family of fourteen quite adequately on a modest and single income.

Besides giving Mom the freedom to shop when it's most advantageous (it's really dumb to wait until you have to have the item and pay full price), being a provider means doing things for her that she can't readily do for herself. One good example is that of providing a suitable facility for her working and teaching. Jesus said He was going *to prepare a place* for His bride, and we have that responsibility as well. My sons and I have had to be creative because of the normal size of our house and the abnormal size of our family. We built a shoe shelf (it looks like a big bookcase with dividers) in the basement entryway, floored the attic for storage, installed a pull-down attic stairway, hung ceiling fans to augment the air conditioning (they also teach children not to play trampoline on the beds), built extra shelves in the closets, enclosed the carport, and performed a number of other fun activities. Providing a place for your wife means making your home as suitable as possible a setting for her work. It you've had to work in unsuitable surroundings or with inferior equipment you should be able to sympathize.

A sometimes-neglected aspect of providing for one's family is preparation for the children's future careers. By that I don't mean college, although that may be a part of the plan. I'm more concerned with teaching our children a useful way to make a living than with giving them a free ride through the hallowed halls. Of my own sons, the three who are old enough to do so have all been apprenticed in our family construction business and are capable workmen by age sixteen or seventeen. In addition, they work with Marilyn and me in the work of producing and distributing our books. When we do a seminar or convention, we are assisted by one or more of the boys and more recently twelve-year-old Katie.

In addition to discipleship in the parents' work, a father can provide opportunities for his children to pursue their own interests and develop talents in areas unrelated to what the rest of the family is doing. Our eldest son Rick, at nineteen, is an avid political activist and is working as a volunteer for a Congressional candidate in our home district. Last spring he was elected county chairman of our party, making him the youngest county chairman in the state. Number two son Tim is a mechanical type who works full time for me and then puts in another three hours or so six days a week as maintenance man for our church.

I couldn't have taught either politics or fix-it work, but I've encouraged the boys over the years to follow their natural bents and it is paying off being involved in the business of the family and the community also has the important benefit of teaching children the skills of business and human relationships.

Function #2: Disciplinarian

HEBREWS 12:11 *If ye endure chastening, God dealeth with you as with sons; for what son is he whom the father chasteneth not?* KJV

In my experience there is no more common cause for home-education burnout than uncontrollable children. Moms are throwing up their hands, pleading personality conflicts, incompatibility, fallen arches or some other malady and putting the children back in school. Unless God has made mistakes and placed children in the wrong families, the supposed personality clashes are in fact something else. It may be that what is needed is for Mom and Dad to get together and agree on some standards of behavior and procedures for their enforcement. To avoid the 'two masters' syndrome, consistency is critical. Ultimately though, God puts the responsibility for child discipline on the father. He must make sure the children know that to disobey Mom is to disobey Dad and they will incur consequences.

Function #3: Teacher

PROVERBS 4:1 *Hear, ye children, the instruction of a father, and attend to know understanding.* KJV

Yes, Dad is to be his children's teacher. But to construe that to mean that he has to be in the "classroom" with them between nine and noon is to betray a very narrow definition of teaching. Most fathers are not available during the morning hours and there is no need for them to be. Rather, we need to learn that learning happens at all hours of the day and how to take advantage of both planned and unplanned teaching opportunities. If Dad's schedule does happen to permit him to be in on the structured teaching time or give some regular time to the task after work in the evening, it may indeed be appropriate for him to teach one or more of the standard subjects from the standard textbooks. That's fine, if he can manage it and the children enjoy it. After all, if the father has more expertise in math or science or history than Mom, why shouldn't the kids get the benefit? But there is much he can do to contribute to the educational process beyond that obvious option and the family will be the richer for his cultivation of those opportunities.

Dad should be involved in the planning of the curriculum. My wife says that the best thing I can do to help her teach our children is to take her out to dinner. As you can imagine, it's not easy around our house to carry on a thoughtful and extended conversation. Marilyn swears that we are at our most creative when facing each other over a restaurant table. And it is at those times that we have some of our best discussions about what we want to teach our children and how to go about it. Fortunately, curriculum development works as well at the cheaper places as anywhere else.

Dad also can be active in support functions such as reviewing work with the children, discussing textbook questions, and taking part in extra study projects such as encyclopedia searches, library trips, etc. Field trips are a good opportunity for the father's involvement too, but beware of joining other families for this. Many support groups fall into the schoolish pattern of doing field trips en masse, resulting in a phenomenon that resembles a learning excursion not so much as a buffalo stampede.

Incidental learning is a fun and profitable opportunity for dads as well. There are all sorts of situations from which education can be harvested with a little effort and creativity. Take the kids out in a rain shower to observe erosion in the garden (the smaller ones will love it).

Dissect a chicken from the grocery store—or better, a freshly killed one from a farm. Plant something exotic in the flower bed. I once found a dead (but not too dead) raccoon on the road and brought it home to show the boys. We skinned it, dissected it and tried to identify some body parts. I was pretty sure about heart, lungs, stomach and kidneys but there were some pretty nondescript objects in there so pancreas, gizzard, pistons, transistors, etc., had to go unlabeled. The boys thought it fascinating so they hung the carcass in a tree to show to the neighbors.

The Father's Role Chapter 9

Function #4: Motivator

1 Thesselonians 2:11 *As ye know how we exhorted
and comforted and charged every one of you, as a
father **doth** his children.* KJV (emphasis mine)

From time to time Mom may call for help in getting the children to give their best efforts or for a little encouragement for herself. At these times Dad can come in very handy. Without getting into an in-depth exposition (which would be beyond mv depth), let's look at what the verse says about the three motivational responsibilities of a father.

Exhort in this text comes from a Greek word meaning to call near, to beseech, to urge. This word is related to the one used to describe the encouraging work of the Holy Spirit. The word translated "comfort" means essentially that very thing: to speak near, to comfort. The emphasis seems to be on sensitivity to the child's needs and sympathy for his pain. To *charge* means literally, to testify. I gather this means that there is value in a father's teaching his children from his own observation and experience. All three terms bespeak close personal contact in terms of intensity of relationship and physical proximity. It seems to be the father's job to stay in close touch with the emotional and spiritual needs of his children and supply encouragement, comfort, and the benefit of his experience.

Dad can perform these three motivational functions in a variety of ways, most of which aren't complicated or time consuming. Taking the time to talk with them about what they are learning (formally or informally), listening to their reading or other assignments, offering rewards for extra effort, correcting their workbooks,

Chapter 9 The Father's Role

looking up things with them in dictionaries or encyclopedias, going to the library together—these are a few of an endless list of little things that have big results when woven into a pattern of loving involvement. All such little efforts provide morsels of learning and more importantly, they all tell the child you care.

Function #5: Leader

> 1 Corinthians 11:1: *Be ye followers of me, even as I also am of Christ.* kjv

> Genesis 18:19 *For I know him, that he will command his children and his household after him, and they shall keep the way of the Lord, to do justice and judgment; that the Lord may bring upon Abraham that which he hath spoken of him.* kjv

One of the greatest causes of insecurity to a wife is a husband who doesn't exhibit leadership. True, a woman can kill initiative in her husband by constantly second-guessing him and complaining about the results of his decisions, but still God holds the man of the house primarily responsible for the direction the family takes. In our day we have seen an epidemic of fathers without leadership. A consequence of this epidemic has made itself felt in church leadership. One of the qualifications for elders that is mentioned in both New Testament lists (*see* 1 Timothy 3:4 and Titus 1:6) is effective leadership in the home. Presumably because candidates who meet this requirement are scarce in our day, many churches have lowered their standards to accept as leaders men who wouldn't have passed muster in times past. The result is a mass of churches which, like their leaders, lack God's power and so fail to demonstrate to a skeptical society that our God is the answer to their needs.

The family seems to be God's boot camp for leaders. The Old Testament judge Samuel, though he was a great and godly man in many ways, failed to lead his own sons to godliness. That failure resulted not only in the end of his role as the highest leader in the land, but also the transition of Israel from a theocracy to a monarchy. Samuel's failure in his family translated into disaster for a much broader spectrum of people, and the same thing happens more often than we like to admit in the modern church and society at large.

For the serious home-educating family, the role of the father as a leader is critical. There are a number of important questions to be resolved during the course of the childrearing years, and failure to address them wisely and decisively can be the ruin of individuals and families. How shall we educate our children? A dad needs to examine the options and take a stand on home education if he concludes, as I have, that Scripture requires it for our family. What are our standards for behavior? What church should we attend? How involved should we be in church? Where should we live'? How should we structure our family ministry? What should be our standards for courtship and marriage? How will we conduct the spiritual training of our children? How should we earn our living? The list goes on and on.

Wives and children need strong fathers to lead them. No dad is perfect and mistakes, although regrettable, are unavoidable. But worse than a bad decision is a needful decision left unmade. Families are hesitant to follow a man who makes too many bad decisions, but it is impossible to follow a man who will not take the responsibility to make decisions at all.

Function #6: Father

> PSALM 127:3–5 *Lo, children are an heritage of the* LORD: *and the fruit of the womb* **is his** *reward. As arrows* **are** *in the hand of a mighty man; so* **are** *children of the youth. Happy* **is** *the man that hath his quiver full of them: they shall not be ashamed, but they shall speak with the enemies in the gate.* KJV

Parents of large families are often asked why they chose to have *so many* children. In our case, the answer is that we didn't choose. We felt that the LORD was more likely to do a wise job of planning our family than we were and so we left it with Him.

God's plan for the human race has always involved multiplying a godly seed. Hence His repeated commands and promises concerning multiplying. Satan's program, on the other hand, has always been to exterminate the godly seed. Hence, Pharaoh's command to drown the baby boys and later Herod's to slaughter the children of Judea below two years of age.

I realize that our philosophy flies in the face of conventional wisdom and for the average parent it's a bit hard to swallow. Parenting a large family is a big responsibility and a lot of work. For Marilyn and me it has meant continuing to bring children into our home while many of our contemporaries are sending theirs out of the home. Our oldest and youngest children are nearly twenty years apart in age. That would seem to many to be a tremendous age spread, but on the other hand, our oldest son is, next to Mom, the favorite family member of the youngest. There are a number of other benefits to a large family, but I don't think I'll change anybody's mind about family planning in the space allotted here. Drop in sometime and we'll talk about it.

An old German proverb says it well:

Many children make many prayers, and many prayers bring much blessing.

It could be mentioned as well that many children (and grandchildren, etc.) make many votes, many letters to the editor, and many calls to legislators. One of the Biblical functions of a father is, after all, to father children.

Function #7: Protector

MATTEW 12:29 *Or else how can one enter into a strong man's house, and spoil his goods, except he first bind the strong man? and then he will spoil his house.* KJV

If God is our pattern as dads—and He does refer to Himself as our Father—then it would behoove us to look at how He deals with us and learn to deal with our children accordingly. He provides an interesting glimpse into His heart through a number of Scriptures relating to His role as our *Protector*. I once did a quick concordance search and found that God refers to Himself (in the King James version) as a *fortress* 7 times, a *defense* 8 times, a *shield* 13 times, a *refuge* 14 times, and a *rock* 39 times. Does that sound like a protective father to you?

Some people are actually offended by home-educators because we exhibit such Neanderthal behavior as sheltering our children. Beware, they say. You'll make your child dependent on you if you keep him with you too much of the time.

Oh, dear. What is the world coming to when children depend on their parents? One problem with the insidious threat of parent-dependency is that its usual alternative is peer-dependency. Numerous studies have been done by institutions ranging from the University of Michigan to Cornell to the Smithsonian, and the evidence overwhelmingly indicates that children are better off with their families than with that famous brotherhood reverently referred to as Kids Their Own Age. How many children ever developed as many bad habits, rebellious attitudes, and unhealthy relationships at home as they have among Kids Their Own Age?

When confronted with all the potential disaster to which I expose my children because I shelter them at home rather than turning them loose in a peer group, I sometimes respond with a question. I ask the concerned citizen to list what he considers to be the five greatest social problems in our country. AIDS? Violence? Teen pregnancy? Drugs? Divorce? Gangs? Illiteracy? There are quite a few to choose from. Once the list of five has been selected, I then ask my companion how many of those five he can trace to the root cause of children spending too much time at home? Er, uh…

Put in the context of the Christian family and home education in particular, the father has his work cut out for him if he takes the protection of his family seriously. There are physical dangers such as exposure to sickness (church nurseries are hotbeds for infections), street violence, and a multitude of trauma for which children seem to be magnets. I could tell you about a trick I did on my bike one time...

Spiritual dangers are both the most important and the most insidious. Wrong friends, bad reading material, television, bestial vibrations (misnamed music), occult toys (or toys that teach materialism and sensuality, e.g. Barbie), all are being used by Satan to attack Christian children. It takes tremendous vigilance and more than a little insight to root out the garbage that can sneak into our children's environment, but it's a necessary effort. By the way, don't forget the educational environment of your children as a source of danger. I consider mass schooling—along with television and contemporary music to be one of the three things most responsible for the moral hemorrhage of this country.

Perhaps even more critical than protecting his children is the father's function in sheltering his wife. Home-educating moms are under special attack because there is no human institution that Satan hates more than the family. If he can damage a mother's physical, spiritual or emotional condition, then he has established an important foothold in the home.

Specifically, women need to be protected in regard to their time. It takes time to teach a five-year-old to read, change a diaper, nurse a baby, cook a meal, or discuss a science project. Yet many moms fail in home

Chapter 9 The Father's Role

education; not because it takes so much time but because there are so many distractions from spending their time wisely. Protecting a wife may mean installing an answering machine, limiting the family's social life, or saying no to a field trip with the support group. Outside activities and interests have a place, but usually not nearly as much *place* as is given to them. You can't home educate if you're never home. It is the husband's responsibility to take the pressure that would otherwise fall on his wife when she puts her family first and invests the amount of time that the job deserves.

On a related subject, a woman needs to be protected emotionally. It's not uncommon for a mom to grow discouraged with home education just because she feels the responsibility is all on her shoulders. She needs time alone with her husband (as I said, Marilyn recommends time in a restaurant) to discuss the needs of the children, hash out problems, and generally just to be assured that he knows and cares what's going on in the home. Protecting Mom emotionally may mean some pretty new maternity outfits when she feels fat and ugly. It may mean keeping her away from all the "Job's wife" types in the world (and sometimes in the church) who are ready and generous with their predictions of tragedy if Mom doesn't do everything right (a standard that nobody, including Mrs. Job, ever attains) in rearing and teaching her children. And once in a while protecting Mom emotionally means shelling out for flowers or chocolates or a new piece of jewelry. If necessary, Dad, carry a bullet in your pocket so you'll have one to bite when the need arises.

Conclusion

If you're looking for a good investment, may I suggest you consider investing in your family. Any investment in human lives is profitable, but it is the seed a man sows in the lives of his wife and children that produces the greatest eternal harvest. Legion is the name of the modern American father who is so busy making a living for his family that he has no time left to make a life for them, because he is many. May he learn before it is too late that he can spend the needful time now in cultivating his kids, or much more time later trying to patch up the results of problems that could have been avoided. Or worse yet, spend the rest of his life in regret.

The state of Christian manhood in our day isn't pretty, but there is an encouraging stirring among the dry bones. Nowhere is the rattling more audible than in the home-education movement, where men are gradually moving back into leadership in their families, churches and support groups. It is in the home-education arena that old stereotypes are most quickly going the way of old snakeskin as a new breed of hands-on dad emerges. He is a man who, given the choice, would rather spend a Saturday fishing with his son than golfing with his boss. His priorities, his loyalties, and his definition of manhood are different from those of the hollow men around him. He is man enough to be different and be different without apology.

The great human enterprise began with God and one man. God saw that it was not good for man to be alone and took steps to correct things. But what an empty picture that day of creation would have been had the woman and the child come first. God made food before He made human stomachs so that His people could have the supply before the need. Likewise, God made man before the family because He knew that the crying need of a woman and her children will always be a hands-on dad. A man; present, caring, involved.

God's creation plan goes on today. His plan for the family goes on as well. And the message men are once again hearing is the same one that man heard in the hopeful birth year of the race, when the voice of the Father harmonized with the plea of every wife and child who would ever live: Dad, we need you.

Chapter 10
Socialization

WITHOUT A DOUBT, the issue of social development is the most common challenge put forth by the critics of home education. Partially for that reason, it's the area in which home educators have gone to the greatest lengths to compensate. And the vast majority of people on both sides of the question have it all wrong.

Schoolists say that home educators are depriving their children of healthy social contact by withdrawing them from daily exposure to kids their own age. Untrue. Home educators respond that they can meet their children's social needs quite adequately by involving them in Little League, scouts, church youth activities and the like. Also untrue.

The fact of the matter is that the family is God's chosen social group for children. Age peer groups have been shown by reams of research to be the worst age arrangement in terms of social learning. To replace a school peer group with a collection of other groups to compensate for lost contact with kids their own age is like replacing a rattlesnake with four copperheads. The poison isn't as potent, but with more sources perhaps you can make up the difference.

When I wrote *The Socialization Trap* I was accused by at least one reviewer of having given disproportionate attention to the negative side of the subject and too little time to the positives of how to socialize children. So what did they expect from a book with that title? It's called *The Socialization Trap*, not *The Socialization Banana Split*, for Pete's sake. It was intended to be a critical look at age peer social grouping and what it's done to our society, and therefore why we as home educators shouldn't use it as a model for socializing our children which is precisely what most home educators do. The main purpose of the book was to tell home educators to stop doing what they were doing because it was bad.

The other reason that the book gave so little space to the positive side of socialization is that it needs little space. Yes, that's right. The development of social attitudes is not complicated and doesn't require submerging children into a giant, elaborate, contrived social environment. Don't be among the unwise parents who take their children out of school, often precisely because of the negative effects of the peer group, and then invest a tremendous amount of time and energy in building a new peer group for them outside school.

The first of two cold, hard facts you must learn about social development is this: *Age peer social environments are bad for children.* That's hard for a lot of people to swallow because 1.) Our society has grouped children by age for so many generations that it seems normal to us, and 2.) We are so often challenged on our children's *lack* of social opportunity that we tend to grow defensive and compensate although no compensation is needed.

The second cold, hard fact to be learned is this: *God designed the family to be the basic social unit in which children learn to live with others.* Think for a minute how many centuries went by before children began to grow up in environments anything like the mass education systems of today. They are strictly a twentieth century phenomenon. In the schools of the 1800's children only went to school a few months of the year and many, because of the western expansion of our population, only for a year or two or not at all. At the turn of the century we were still only up to about ten percent in public school attendance. And until the consolidation movement of recent decades not just classes, but in fact schools themselves, were much smaller, allowing for community control and a far more personal environment. As recently as the middle of this century, children spent much more time at home, were much more dependent on their parents, and had closer ties to siblings and the extended family. It shouldn't be forgotten that we had a much healthier society then.

The socialization issue is representative of how we tend to model home education after schools. We have rejected school for our children, yet are so habituated to parts of it that we find it hard to shed the presuppositions. But shed them we must, and the first one that needs to go on the ash heap is the idea that children need Kids Their Own Age for a social group. That's why I wrote *The Socialization Trap*. One lady told me that her mother-in-law had vehemently opposed the home education of her grandchildren until the daughter-in-law gave her the *Trap* to read. She returned it a few days later saying, "That's all I needed to know. By all means, take the kids out of school." That sort of thing makes my day.

If you've not yet heard of Dr. Raymond Moore, you will. From the research point of view Dr. Moore is probably the world's preeminent authority on home education. He was interviewed in *Human Events* magazine in 1984 and had some encouraging things to say on the ability of the family to form social skills:

This pervasive idea that children are better socialized and adjusted if they are constantly surrounded by their peers is an extravagant myth. You know there is positive socialization and negative socialization. The child who has been taught at home, who feels needed and wanted, who knows he is depended on at home—sharing responsibilities and chores is much more likely to develop a sense of self worth and a stable value system which is the basic ingredient for a positive sociability.

We know now that the child that is with his peers more than with his parents at least until the age of 12 will become peer-dependent and negatively socialized. There are so many studies to support that—Urie Brontenbrenner's studies at Cornell, the Albert Bandura studies from Stanford.

Dr. Bronfenbrenner says that the child who is peer-dependent loses a crucial sense of self-worth—a desperate loss. He loses his optimism and is much less self-directed than he should be; he loses trust for his parents, and, ultimately, loses respect for his peers as well. What does a child have left then? There you have an almost perfect profile of the rebels of the sixties and the drug and sex culture of the seventies.

An article published in the Phi Delta Kappan in March, 1983, reported a comparison of more than a thousand schools and found that the average amount of time spent in person-to-person responses between teachers and students amounted to seven minutes a day. That means if your child is one of twenty or thirty youngsters in a classroom and the teacher is giving only seven minutes a day in responses, that your child is lucky if he gets spoken to once a day. There will be a certain amount of communication between him and the other students, but this is extremely limited by *quiet classroom* rules and besides, we've already pointed out the inferiority of peer social contact. When he is learning at home with you, he may get direct input and answers from you two or three hundred times in a day. There are intellectual benefits from age integration, too. A respected UNC psychologist, Harold McCurdy, says that genius is derived from the experience of children being most of the time with adults and very little with their peers. A recent Smithsonian study found the same thing to be true. That means that the herding together of children by age group in schools is the wrong road to achievement.

This is borne out by the experience of John Quincy Adams, sixth president of the United States. Because his father was a diplomat, John Quincy moved from nation to nation as a child and spent the vast majority of his time in the company not of peers, but of brilliant and prominent adults. He was only fourteen when he received a Congressional appointment as secretary to America's foreign minister to Russia. Presumably he was a bright boy. And if he was a social misfit, nobody seemed to notice.

The Hewitt Research Foundation did a study of 400 adults who were taught at home and found that nearly all were now leaders in their professions or trades and were remarkably successful parents. Another survey of home-taught adults showed that over two-thirds of them owned

Chapter 10 **Socialization**

their own businesses. This goes to show that a person's ability to get along with others doesn't depend on having enough time with Kids Their Own Age. A look at the lives of those who grew up free of age segregation is a better indicator than the dire predictions of conventional wisdom and pop psychology.

God created families for children; man created age peer grouping. Once again we find that God's way works. In Bible times, and in our own not-so-distant past as a nation, generations of families often lived for a lifetime in the same communities and sometimes in the same house. Respect for elders was a given, and parents had the benefit of their own parents' support in rearing their children. The importance of respect for the aged and for one's parents is demonstrated by the fact that the Old Testament penalty for rebellion against one's parents was death by stoning (DUETERONOMY 21:18–21).

Today we've gone to about the limit in the opposite direction. That this can be a problem is demonstrated by the history of Nazi Germany. During the 1930's Hitler encouraged children to look directly to him, rather than their parents for leadership. The upshot of this was the Hitler Youth, a paramilitary organization complete with Swastika arm bands. Hitler taught that disrespect for old age was a form of weakness. I can't prove this, but I suspect that some of the atrocities by the Hitler Youth against Jews and others would have been harder to bring about had those children and teenagers followed their parents' leadership rather than Hitler's. I find it hard to believe that the average German family was as vicious as Hitler.

In our country we are fragmenting society by separating old people from others by mothballing them in Florida while incarcerating the young in schools where they are separated from parents and even siblings through age grading. As I've said before, we've come to accept this as normal through habituation but our society has suffered for it.

Peer Socialization

In Chapter 3 of *The Socialization Trap* I enunciate five reasons that peer-group social learning is unhealthy. I reproduce them here to round out a picture of the negative side of the question before we discuss the positive how-to's of building social skills in your children. I hope they will supply you with some ammunition next time you're attacked on the need of your children for more contact with kids their own age.

1. Peer socialization tends to make children dependent on their peers for values.

I found a college sociology text, circa 1986, that provided an eye-opening picture of the modern liberal view of what peer groups are all about:

> *The peer group helps children form attitudes and values. It provides a filter for sifting through their parent-derived values and **deciding which ones to keep and which to discard*** (italics added).

Unfortunately, the authors are exactly correct. That is precisely what peer groups do for children. The

Chapter 10 **Socialization**

frightening thing about it is that the authors were saying this approvingly, evidently on the assumption that it is entirely proper and healthy for children to toss their parents' values overboard if the consensus of their ten- or twelve-year-old colleagues so dictates. They continued:

> *Peer groups often impose their values on the emerging individual. Children play games in groups... Unfortunately it's usually in the company of friends that children also shoplift, begin to smoke and drink, sneak into the movies, and do other undesirable things. Sixth graders who are rated as more peer-oriented report engaging in more of this kind of behavior than parent-oriented children...*

Their words, not mine. And yet they acknowledged no possibility that we should even think of limiting the amount of time children spend in groups of their peers.

Peer addiction is every bit as powerful as an addiction to nicotine. We think with a mixture of pity and distaste of the poor smoker who wakes in the wee hours needing a cigarette and, unable to locate his pack in the dark, pokes around in a dirty ashtray in hopes of finding a butt long enough to light without scorching the end of his nose. I've reached the point where I'm just as shocked and saddened when I see children or teenagers so addicted to the approval of their peers that they engage in behavior that grieves their parents, damages their health and/or just makes them look like idiots.

Smoking itself is a good example of such behavior. Hardly anybody starts smoking as an adult because we know it invites cancer, wastes money, causes bad breath and tastes terrible. But while the percentage of adults who smoke is declining, more children are starting than ever before. Part of this could reasonably be blamed on advertising. Some of the newer billboard ads appear to be slanted more toward children. Still, smoking is unpleasant at first and it seems doubtful that advertising alone would ever convince most children to start. It takes the pressure of a dare, the fear of contempt from peers to turn most youngsters into nicotine addicts.

2. Peer socialization subjects children to constant attacks on their self-esteem.

Quoting again from the aforementioned sociology text,

> *The peer group provides children with a more realistic gauge for the development of skills and abilities than the parents, who are so much bigger and wiser and more powerful, or than baby brothers and sisters. Only within a **large** group of peers can children get a sense of how smart, how athletic, how skillful and how personable they are.* (italics added)

In other words, peer groups perform the *essential* function of teaching our children to assess their own worth in terms of *how they compare with others*. I admit to being entirely at a loss as to how this constant comparison and competition is going to help children. It seems to me to be the antithesis of the assurances of Scripture that we are all important individuals uniquely created by God, as described in Psalm 139. The fact is that everybody is inferior to someone else in any number of ways. God never intended for us all to be the same, but for each of us to make the most of the raw material He has placed within us. To base our self-esteem on what we can do compared with what others can do is assurance that we will never measure up entirely.

One of the common arguments for subjecting children to the peer pressure of school is that they are getting ready to enter a world full of pressure and need to *get used to it*. That's wrong. On the contrary, children in schools are already in the world of pressure, and most of them will face much less pressure, at least socially, as adults. When I was a schoolboy I moved daily in an environment where my physical safety was threatened by bigger boys needing to prove their machismo, where verbalizing a wrong answer could bring howls of scornful laughter and where the rudest contempt was regularly heaped on those who did poorly on tests, or couldn't run as fast as others on the playground. Rudeness, bullying, exclusion, mockery, and cliques were the order of the day. To say that is good for a child's soul or mind is tantamount to saying that eating garbage will make his body healthy.

It's also silly to say that it prepares a child for the *real world*. I live in the real world, and people don't act that way here. Anyone who did would stand a good chance of losing his friends, job, and any degree of respect in the eyes of the community. Yet in school society such obnoxiousness is business as usual.

3. Peer socialization fosters negative attitudes toward other age groups.

It is normal, natural, and Biblical for humans to have reverence for the old and tenderness toward the young. Yet these traits are steadily disappearing from the American psyche. Old people are seen as fossils of a bygone era who are no longer of value except as relics. Babies and toddlers are shuttled off to day care centers and preschools with hardly a thought that they might actually miss their mommies.

In other societies, this isn't always the case. In the former Soviet Union, for instance, teenage boys will hug and kiss little children they hardly know, and do so in public. As Dr. Bronfenbrenner (in his book, *The Two Worlds of Childhood*) points out, similar behavior on the part of an American teenage boy would send his parents in search of psychiatric help for him immediately.

As for respect for the aged, I can recall in my own growing up years that there was a social obligation to refer to one's parents as Old Man and Old Lady when in the company of peers. Adults wore loose pants when pants were supposed to be tight, listened to country or classical music when it was generally understood that only rock'n'roll was acceptable and otherwise betrayed the fact that they were far down the chute of irrelevance. The idea of asking an old person's opinion about the weighty matters of growing up was unheard of

That's a great shame. We told ourselves as adolescents that we were at the top of the food chain, the pinnacle of centuries-long social evolution. But I knew, and I suspect we all knew, that the teen years were a time of terrible self doubt and insecurity. We were struggling with questions of right and wrong, wise and unwise, profitable and unprofitable. Now I look back and say: if only I had listened… In fact, I should have been asking.

4. Peer socialization breaks down family relationships

The time factor alone can separate a school child from his family to a tremendous extent. Think for a minute about the average child's schedule on a school day. He would probably get up about 6:30AM, dress, eat breakfast and otherwise get ready for school, catch the bus at 7:30 and be at school around 8:00. He is in school until 3 or 3:30PM. After that, especially if he is in junior or senior high school, he may have sports practice, play rehearsal, music lessons, or other extracurricular commitments. Since his mother probably works, even if he is home by 4:00PM, it may be another hour or so before the child sees either of his parents. In the evening he may (or may not) do an hour or two of homework, but statistically most of his time will be spent in front of the television, as will that of his parents. The average American, studies say, watches about fifty hours a week.

During my senior year in high school, I got this process down to a science. I found that if I got involved in enough activities, I could have something interesting to do most of the time and Mom didn't think to ask me about homework. I guess she assumed that since I was spending so much time at school I must be working hard. So after school I had sports practice until 5:30PM, then I might go home for supper and be back at school for play practice at 7:00. I'd get home at 10 or 11:00PM, at which time I'd collapse into bed. The next day would be a repeat, right up to the weekend. Some nights I would substitute a sports event for play practice. Then on weekends I'd frequently be out with friends, away at a debate, or at a forensics tournament. All in all, I was seldom with my family—

and when I was, the glowing blue tube kept us more or less distracted.

So just the time commitment that revolves around school can be a major factor in damaging family relationships. And I could have added that the bizarre modern phenomenon of quota busing adds to the problem, sometimes doubling or tripling the amount of time a child spends on the way to or from school.

But beyond the mechanical fact of physical separation due to the time factor, the emotional effects of peer-group life tend to weaken family ties. It's amazing how quickly peer pressure can affect what were formerly strong relationships at home.

A few years ago a couple came to us for some help in starting to home educate. They had just moved to our city from rural Pennsylvania, where the father had been the headmaster of a small and apparently very good Christian school. On moving to our area they had enrolled their children in a large and well-known Christian school and felt that everything was in order. Before the school year was half over they were seeing problems. The straw that broke the camel's back was an incident that happened after church one evening. Mom had gone to the nursery to pick up her two-year-old son. On the way out of the building she passed a group of boys including her fifteen-year-old son and some of his school friends. The younger son was very fond of his older brother, so when his mother carried him past the boys in the hall, he leaned out from her arms and reached out for his brother to take him. The older boy quickly turned his back and went on talking with his friends, pretending he hadn't noticed. The two-year-old was heartbroken.

Chapter 10 **Socialization**

The parents were of course hurt by this, and shocked that in only a few months their teenager could be so influenced by his peers' contempt for younger siblings that he could treat his little brother so coldly. It didn't take long for them to make up their minds about home education.

Another man told me that when he started high school his parents had arranged for him to ride to school with his older brother, who was also a student there and drove his car each day. The brother protested that it wasn't cool to drive to school with one's drippy younger sibling, but the parents were adamant. As they approached the school on the first morning his brother told him to crawl over into the backseat and hide on the floor until the car had stopped and the older boy had been out of the car for a count of one hundred. All this subterfuge was deemed necessary because of the tremendous amount of negative social pressure on sibling relationships.

Some parents have bought into the myth that children need to be entirely independent of their parents. Even some home-education writers have suggested that children be allowed to decide as early as kindergarten age whether they will attend school or be taught at home. I strongly disagree with that. God gave children parents for some reason, and if feeding and clothing them were the extent of it, then the government would be correct in its modern approach of trying to take over childrearing from families. But our generation is pretty brainwashed and it will take some time to reverse the process.

Marilyn and I once chatted over dinner with a couple who had a fourteen-month-old baby. His mother commented that she was looking for a sitter for the child because he was "getting too attached to Mama" by spending all his time with her. Dear me, a baby who's attached to his mother. What's the world coming to? I don't believe that was her real reason, of course. She was less concerned about making Baby free of Mama than she was about making Mama free of the Baby. But just the fact that she could advance such an argument as justification and expect nobody to laugh out loud testifies to how little value our society places on family bonding. That's the extent to which our own age-segregated upbringing has brainwashed us.

5. Peer socialization isolates children from the real adult world.

The history of civilization has demonstrated that children are by nature interested in the activities of adults. That is as it should be. We see it every day in our toddlers and preschoolers. You can't go into another room and close the door without hearing *Mommy!* yelled at you from without before half a minute goes by. *Whatcha doing?* is also a favorite salutation.

But there comes a time in a modern child's life when he no longer exhibits that fascination with what adults are doing. I don't know the average age at which it becomes evident, but it seems to me that before junior high or at least high school, most young people have stopped studying the behavior of their elders and centered their interest in what their peers are doing. This is a tragedy, because it means that children are losing their interest in adult life as they get closer to having to live it. Think of the difference between a toddler accompanying his mother on her Saturday morning rounds. Mom drops by the post office and Junior must drop the letters through the slot. Mom stops by the bank and Junior asks a hundred questions in five minutes. Mom picks up some groceries and Junior wants to know what everything is throughout the entire store.

Visualize what the trip would have been like had Junior been a high school senior. He would have stayed in the car and listened to the radio during all three stops. The irony is that Junior the toddler, the one burning with curiosity and eagerness, is fifteen years away from having to do for himself the things he's doing with Mom today while Junior the seventeen-year-old may very well be living in an apartment of his own or away at college within a year. He is the one who very soon may need to use the post office, do his own banking, and shop for the best buys. The boy who needs the experience with Mom the most, wants it least.

Where did Junior's interest go between age three and age seventeen? It went down the rathole of adolescence. Junior lives in a society that keeps him, for most of his waking hours, out of communication with adults and out of touch with their business. Until graduation dumps him into the marketplace, workplace and community, he sees little of what goes on there, and so understands little of its importance. Meanwhile the artificial environment of American adolescence supplies him with a variety of obligations and entertainments to absorb his time, interest and energy, thus ensuring that he is ever less likely to stick his head out of the cocoon. I wonder how many high school seniors have shared the experience of shock I had on graduation night when it dawned on me that suddenly it was all over?

There's much more to this phenomenon than the material structure of the system that so segregates adolescents from the other age groups. It's the spiritual and emotional side of the scenario that is both interesting and disturbing. The environment of school and its related activities, the other common age-segregated pastimes such as scouts, little league, church programs etc., keeps young people from being available to involvement in the larger world, but the spiritual/emotional effect of years of living this way is a loss of interest in the larger world. Give the average teenager a choice between attending a school dance and a political rally, and you'll see what I mean.

Sensible Socializing

Assuming that you're now satisfied that *normal* socialization is bad, the next step is to develop a positive approach to the development of social skills. It's not all that hard. The difficult part is protecting your children from the inducements of taking part in every age-graded activity concocted by your church, support group or who ever. If you manage to detach them from the counterproductive, providing them with the productive doesn't take a lot of engineering.

First, start with the family. That, as I keep repeating, is God's basic social group. It is in the family that the first, most important, and most lasting attitudes toward one's self and others are formed. There are several reasons for this.

Family relationships are intense. Your spouse knows you so well you can hardly get away with anything and it's partly because you spend so much time together. The same applies between parent and child, and child and siblings. They say the true test of friendship is to survive being roommates and this applies doubly to family. For some reason we seem to have less hesitation to lash out at family members and less tolerance for their failings. Family members see one another at the best and worst times and have to learn to accept each other through all seasons. That's why the family is the boot camp for learning to get along with non-relatives, all of whom have failings as well.

Family relationships are diverse. This is not as true in small families as in large ones, but God arranges for each of us to have the parents and siblings who will be just right for building our character. Some of that comes through their example and encouragement to us, some of it comes through meeting each other's needs and some of it comes by rubbing each other the wrong way. We can't correct our faults if we can't see them, and God knows what personality types to put together in a family to bring those faults conveniently into the light.

Family relationships are guided. Children aren't just tossed together without supervision as on a playground, but placed in a home with loving parents who serve as examples, counselors, and sometimes referees. Problems don't have to go unresolved if they're beyond the children's ability; Mom and Dad step in and help work things out.

Family relationships are interdependent. Parents are not successful if their children are not. Because we aren't in competition but in cooperation with each other, we're all responsible to pull together for the success of each one. The automatic blending of age groups with their varying abilities and needs creates dependence in the younger toward the older members, and sensitivity in the older members toward the younger ones. The needs of one member are often the indicator of needs in another. If a child has a problem with temper for instance, it may be God's cue to one of the parents that a bad example has been set and that his own life needs more self control. If a child is irritated by sharing a room with a messy younger sibling it could be God's cue to develop a teaching relationship with that sibling and help him learn to manage better.

So cultivate your family. Shed some needless time commitments and stay home more. Do more fun things together as a family. Especially if all your children are younger, show them now that home is a fun place before they get driver's licenses and face the kaleidoscope of attractions available to a teen with transportation and a little money. Maintain contact with the extended family, too. Instead of the inane penmanship exercises in the workbooks, assign your children letters to Grandma for writing practice. The same goes for uncles, aunts, and cousins.

Rather than letting your children drift into same-age circles, fellowship as a family with other families who have similar values. This mixes the age groups so that children stay in touch with adult conversation and adults are reminded to cultivate relationships with their friends' children.

Develop a family ministry. It might be visiting in nursing homes, helping disabled or elderly neighbors, or circulating Gospel tracts. Working together as a team cements family ties. In our family, it happens to be a home-education ministry. At any given convention or seminar, Mom or Dad might be speaking in a workshop while the other parent is sharing suggestions with an attendee and one or more of our children distribute handouts or sell books and tapes.

Along this line, learn to think in terms of service-oriented relationships in general. So often we seem to choose our friends and associates based on whose company we enjoy the most. We should rather seek out companions who will influence us to greater Christian growth and whom we can encourage in turn. There's more to friendship than fun. A word of caution, though. Beware of letting your children dabble in danger by forming *ministry* friendships with people who are more likely to drag them down than be lifted up. I know a man whose daughter is a single mother for that very reason.

Encourage your children by word and example to be involved in the business of the real world. If you can, get them involved to some extent in your job or business so they can see what it's like to be a part of the world of work and commerce. Take them with you to political meetings or community projects such as Habitat for Humanity. In general, make them a part of your life outside the home as well as in. That's the most realistic preparation for the time when they have to take on an adult role for themselves. As they move under your guidance throughout the workplace, marketplace, church, neighborhood and greater community, they will come in contact with a wide variety of people of different ages, backgrounds, ethnicities, interests, abilities, experiences, skills, and temperaments. This, starting with the nuclear family, is real socialization.

When it comes to socialization, as well as other things, there is no comparison between school and home education if sensibly done. School is a box in which children are confined with their peers to examine chips of the real world that are passed in through a hatch. Home education is parents taking their children by the hand and leading them out among the wonders of the real world, teaching by experience, instruction and example. And learning with them, which may be the most fun of all.

*For Thou didst form
my inward parts;
Thou didst weave me
in my mother's womb.
I will give thanks to Thee,
for I am fearfully
and wonderfully made;
Wonderful are thy works,
and my soul knows it
very well.*

—PSALM 139:13–14 NASB

Chapter 11
Preparing For A Career

I F THERE IS A STANDARD CONCEPTION of the process of preparing for a career in America, it would have to be the idea of graduating from high school, going to college, getting a degree, possibly attending graduate school, then landing a job and rising to the top of the profession. Most people who start college never graduate with a degree in their original major, but still the image persists of the high school-college-yuppiedom process as the norm or ideal.

It's not much different in home-education circles, although it seems to be less pronounced than elsewhere. Probably the main difference is that we aren't so set on pushing our girls out into the workforce, being more in sympathy than others with the Biblical ideal of women working in the home. Home educators as a class also tend more toward self employment than the general populace. I recall reading about a study of home educated adults and being surprised to note that two-thirds of them were employed in a business of their own.

I'm of the opinion that there is a lot of room for development in the home-educator's attitude toward career preparation. The movement is growing so fast, and so many families are now entering it before their children are old enough to have been in school, that only a small percentage of us have yet faced the season of launching some of our offspring into the world of adult work. We also, as a group, still tend to see a considerable difference between college learning and the learning of earlier years. Many parents feel quite confident to teach their children at home through high school but tremble at the thought of attempting to go farther. I also think we need to take a good, hard look at the realities of life and reflect on the benefits of college compared to its costs and the alternatives available. There are several avenues through which a young person can enter the career field God has chosen for him and it behooves us to keep an open mind.

Considerations In Planning

The first consideration that enters the mind of the average parent when thinking about his child's job future is that of money. How can my child best prepare to land a lucrative job? The second consideration is probably job satisfaction. Many parents are themselves stuck in jobs they would like to leave, and want nothing of the sort to happen to their children. Both these concerns are legitimate and deserve reflection, but God's design for work takes a different approach.

Jesus taught that the way to find one's life is to lose it for his sake. He also told his disciples that the greatest among them would serve the others. The principle we should keep in mind, then, is that our goal in seeking a career is not to find that position in which it seems we can best please ourselves, but that position in which we can best glorify God and be of the most service to others.

The happy consolation is that when we seek to do the best we can for God and others, we are serving our own best interests as well. The man who sees his job as just a source of income will never be enthusiastic about it and so will not have the motivation to make the situation all it can be. On the other hand, the man who sees his work as a calling from God and knows that he is making a real contribution to the happiness and well-being of others is a thousand times more likely to be happy in his work. It has a higher purpose than just providing his survival needs.

God is no fool. He designs individual persons for individual roles. As parents it is important to study our children and help them understand who they are, what their talents are, and what God's direction for them seems to be at each stage of their growing up years. We can't assume that they will follow in Dad's footsteps because Dad is fulfilled in his career, or that a job that is considered desirable by the majority of people will suit them. It will take careful and prayerful thought to discern whom God is making each child to be, and what is the best career route in view of what God is doing.

In some cases it's a cakewalk. Many a girl, discerning early on that her calling was that of homemaker, has simply waited for God to bring the right young man into her life and stayed in her parents' home until he arrived. And sometimes a young person's calling is so evident to him, his family, and those who know him that his direction is set from early on.

This latter scenario was the case of my eldest son. Rickey has been a political activist for several years, as everyone who knew him was well aware. Politics has been not only his strongest interest but just about his only strong interest. Now nineteen years old, he has worked as a volunteer in several campaigns, educated himself to a remarkable degree, captured the county party chairmanship from a seven-year incumbent twice his age, and served as area coordinator for a congressional campaign and one for lieutenant governor. He is still living at home and is currently being considered for a couple of different paying

Chapter II **Preparing For A Career**

positions in political work. He plans on running for office himself as soon as he reaches the legal age requirement.

But it's not always so. I myself have four teenagers, none of whom are as clear as to God's direction for them as their older brother. So I sympathize with you if you are in the same boat. But don't panic if your child is nearing college age and still hasn't lit on a career choice. There's nothing wrong with a son or daughter staying home with the family longer than the usual. As a matter of fact, I intend for all my children to stay home until their marriages, unless God clearly calls them to some work that requires them to leave. That way, they can work in the family business, help train their younger siblings and explore their own future prospects without the financial pressure of maintaining their own household. And yes, in case you're wondering, that's quite satisfactory to the kids.

When thinking about your child's future career there are a number of factors to consider. The basic question is, who is your child? With such a high percentage of adults today stuck in jobs from which they get little or no satisfaction (I've had my share), it should be apparent that a haphazard approach to career choice often leaves the individual in a situation for which he is not suited and may in fact serve only to keep him from having the time and energy to seek out something more appropriate.

This isn't to say that God never intentionally puts a person in a painful job. There are character goals to be reached that sometimes require adversity, and a job can be a wonderful source of adversity. In my own case, God has often used my work situation to supply me with the discipline that I didn't learn growing up. But I don't wish that on my children, so I'm taking the two-pronged preventive measure of trying to teach them self-discipline and help them find their career niche at the same time.

For the purposes of this chapter I'll assume that you're doing a responsible job of teaching character to your sons and daughters so the Lord won't need to place them in jobs that function as torture chambers. Reproof functions aside, then, let me make some suggestions as to how to go about searching for the right career field for your kids.

Remember we're going on the assumption that you want to find the position in which your child can be of the most service to God by serving others. He wants to be of maximum effectiveness, which means he wants a job that will make full use of his strengths and be least affected by his weaknesses. The first step is to analyze what those strengths and weaknesses are.

One of the greatest strengths a person can have is cheerfulness. Scripture says that the joy of the Lord is our strength, so it's perfectly reasonable to look for a career in which your child will be happy. Happy people accomplish more than unhappy people. They put emotional energy into their work that unhappy people waste in regret and wishing. A job that doesn't fit is no more cause for Joy than a shoe that doesn't fit. Regardless of your good intentions, you will never run as fast in ill-fitting shoes.

What is your child's spiritual gift? The motivational gifts, listed in ROMANS 12, represent special drives and abilities that God gives to believers to enable us to meet the needs of others in the name of the Lord. They represent a big part of a person's resources for work and blessed is he who can use his gift every day on the job.

My own gift is exhortation, which more than anything else means encouragement. I love to encourage people and it's been painful for me that most of my work history has involved things more than people. Probably the darkest period of my working life was the five years I spent painting houses. I wrote about those days in my book *Yes, They're All Ours,* so I won't waste your time crying about it here. Suffice it to say that there's not much you can say to a house that will get much of a response out of it.

I love most what I'm doing now, which is working to encourage Christian parents. And because exhortation is a verbally oriented gift I enjoy speaking encouragement most of all. I've found that writing books is work for me, but speaking is fun. When the Lord gives me the opportunity to speak to a group of parents at a seminar or state convention I always have the time of my life. I love to feel that I'm providing a little uplift for Christian moms and dads, whom I admire so much and whose job is both terribly important and quite demanding. Any time I say something before a group that helps one of my listeners see a better way of ministering to his or her children, or that gives new confidence, I feel like a little boy getting a puppy for Christmas. It's pure joy.

If I had my career to start over again, I would have a much more realistic picture of who I am, and what I am and am not good for. I would be praying about jobs in the ministry or, being too immature for that, in teaching or sales or some kind of motivational work. I would try to avoid jobs that majored on *things*, especially those with little people contact and little variety. I would shy away from jobs that required a detail person, because I am oriented toward motivating others rather that fussing around keeping loose ends tied up. I need to deal with living creatures whose makeup includes spirit and emotion. Material things and raw data such as numbers demotivate me. They can't feel anything.

But not everybody is an exhorter. Which is fortunate, because everybody would be trying to motivate everybody else to greatness and nobody would want to take the time to fix the refrigerator. Nobody needs a Maytag man who does nothing but pat you on the shoulder and tell you how confident he is that you can handle this crisis.

Perhaps your child has the gift of serving. Most likely he is a hands-on type who likes to keep those hands moving most of the time. Servers enjoy doing the physical things that keep the operation moving and are a great blessing although they often aren't appreciated as much as they deserve because they tend to function with quiet efficiency. If your child is a server he will more likely be happy in some type of mechanical work rather than an organizational or paper-shuffling role. I would expect him to be more productive as a maintenance engineer or a mechanic than selling insurance.

If your child's gift is ruling, he has a tremendous ability to organize. He is probably good at connecting the right person with the right job and keeping track of the details. The ruler has an eye for the overall operation and is less interested in being a simple cog in some comfortable niche in the machine than being the computer that programs the machine. A person of this type would more likely succeed in management than in an assisting or production role with little opportunity for decision making. He is eager to accept responsibility and is impatient with inefficiency.

What are your child's human talents? Is he musical? Artistic? Inventive? Most people have more than one obvious talent and should be encouraged to consider them all in choosing a career. But remember that it is not only that which we do for money that contributes to the welfare of others and the advancement of God's purposes. If your child loves to ply his fingers on both mechanic's tools and the piano keyboard (as does one of my sons), he may do one for income and the other strictly as a ministry.

Beware of the tendency to settle for second best. If you come to believe that God wants your child in some work that requires years of preparation, encourage him to pay the price and help him in every way you can. We have a son who I think would make a good veterinarian. His gift is showing mercy and he loves animals. But he is hesitant about the expense in time and money of obtaining a veterinary license, and so has sometimes shown less enthusiasm than I would have expected when the subject came up. In such cases it might be helpful to ask, *If you had the ability and the opportunity to do any job in the world, starting tomorrow, what job would you choose?* This might remove the child's mental roadblocks and give a clearer picture of what his deep desire actually is. Once that desire has been identified, begin to pray about it and explore the related possibilities. If there are discouraging obstacles, assure your child that you will help him find ways to overcome them.

It should be remembered that a job is not necessarily a life sentence. It would be lovely if a man could find early on, a job in which he felt that he was just where God wanted him for the rest of his life. But it usually doesn't happen that way. Most men change jobs several times, at least through layoffs or promotions, and many change career fields entirely. You can certainly lose ground that way, especially if you have to enter the new field at the bottom of the totem pole. But some men manage to make each change pay off in the long run, so it's not something to rule out entirely. Besides, there is such a thing as learning to live on less money in order to spend one's days doing something enjoyable and worthwhile instead of just striving for the maximum dollar return.

Help your child do some intelligent exploring. Have him talk to many people in different career fields and find out the pros and cons of each. There are books on the subject in the public library; those might be helpful. Get the counsel of the child's grandparents. God may give them some special insight. The life stories of those who excelled in their jobs may be useful, too. I learned things that have helped me in my business by reading about Sam Walton, Colonel Sanders, and others.

Getting a Start

Once God has shown you and your child a career field whether or not you're satisfied it is for life the question arises as to how to go about entering that field. As I said in the introduction to this chapter, the idea that automatically comes to mind for many people is that of going to college, graduating with honors, and accepting one of a large number of lucrative jobs that will no doubt be offered to your brilliant child. But there are several ways of pursuing a career and they all have advantages and disadvantages to be considered. We'll treat the college issue in a separate chapter, but here let me mention some other possibilities that I think are worth consideration.

Apprenticeship

This is one of the oldest and most effective forms of career training. In fact, it was the primary method of training for most professions until very recent times. Apprenticeship in early America was a set period of time during which a young man would work (and often live) with a skilled professional and serve as his helper without pay in exchange for the job training. It was in this way that Ben Franklin learned the printing trade, apprenticed to his brother at the start of his career.

I think we have yet to scratch the surface of apprenticeship possibilities in the twentieth century. The practical experience of working in the profession could be combined with book study for part of the day. I believe that this combination of hands-on learning and book work may be the cure for the dreadful impracticality and disorientation of today's higher education. Knowledge without application is learning without context.

For instance, what if political science majors studied for a part of the day and worked as volunteers in a campaign or the office of a legislator for the rest of the day? Or how about if pre-med students spent several hours each week working in a hospital or doctor's office?

The ministry is one calling that might benefit more than most by a return to apprenticeship. Charles Finney, the great nineteenth century evangelist, obtained his training in just that way. He was a lawyer when he was converted to Christ, and immediately began sharing the gospel with others. He had a powerful desire to study for the ministry, so his pastor suggested that Finney attend Princeton, where he himself and most of the neighboring pastors had attended school. Young Finney declined his offer of a recommendation, saying that he could see no great good in a Princeton education, since all the ministers in the area were evidently without the power of God in their ministries. He suggested instead that the pastor disciple him, directing him to the best books to study. The minister agreed, and thus Finney was able to benefit from the study of books at the same time as he was involved in the work in the trenches.

Most career fields are making use of apprenticeship principles even now. While some jobs require school diplomas for hiring, practically every job involves some on-the-job training under the eye of more experienced workers. In some cases there is a set term of apprenticeship. A friend of mine worked for a paint contractor who paid him an entry-level wage while he served a three-year apprenticeship including instruction not only in painting, but also plastering, drywall, and wallpaper hanging. I think we will see endless possibilities in apprenticeship if we can ever break out of the habit of separating the learning process from the doing process. It makes so much more sense to combine the two.

Don't get the idea that apprenticeship can be used only to train people in the skilled trades. In my state of Virginia and several other states, even lawyers can get their licenses by this method. They *read law* as an unpaid clerk in a practicing attorney's office, learning the academics while rubbing shoulders every day with the practical application. After three years they're allowed to take the bar exam and if they pass they are licensed to practice law. A friend of mine is a lawyer for the Rutherford Institute, a nonprofit organization created to defend home educators and others prosecuted for their religious beliefs. He went to law school, but he says that reading law is better because it's done in the process of working in the field rather than isolated from it.

Trade schools

This is an option that serves many people well. People enter a wide range of careers through trade schools, which are not like colleges in that they don't offer a liberal arts education, but just training in a particular skill or skills. Some would see this as a disadvantage, especially if what they want from schooling is an exposure to a wide variety of experiences, people, and philosophies. Trade schools exist for the purpose of teaching people a way of making a living. A diploma from such a school is often much more valuable in securing a job than some college degrees, which cover a wide range of majors which are of greater and lesser usefulness in the marketplace.

There are lots of different options in trade school education. Construction, printing, electronics, drafting, welding, auto mechanics, and barbering are among the choices of trades. There are no doubt many others of which I'm not aware, and I suspect that most of them are more valuable in landing a job than a college degree in philosophy. There is usually less cost and less time involved in obtaining a trade school diploma than a college degree. There is also less time wasted if you are concerned about getting a job in the trade of your choice and not in a lot of elective courses. For information on trade schools, ask at your public library.

Family business

If you are in business for yourself it may work very handily for you to move your child or children into it with you as they grow more and more capable. I know a man who started a photo shop after retiring from an executive position with a large company, mainly for the purpose of providing a job for his teenage son. After three years he has two thriving stores. His home-educated son is preparing to take his GED test and enroll in the local community college to take accounting and other courses he will need to take over the business. For that young man, classwork will not be pointless and boring, because he has already spent enough time in the family photo stores to be able to manage one. Because he knows firsthand what knowledge is needed, he will be able to discern what courses and parts of courses are important.

There is one of the great advantages of home education. This boy has been in the business world for three years already and so is equipped to go to college and sift out the valuable material from the fluff. If he had spent those years buried in school, television, sports and entertainment as do most teenagers, he would be going to college blind. His main guide for the comparative value of the courses would be the college catalog.

Having trained my three eldest sons in my drywall business, I'm in a position to know the value of this approach. My boys aren't afraid of work, they have a sense of importance through having learned a man's skills and contributed greatly to the family income, they understand

Chapter 11 Preparing For A Career

the value of hard-earned money, and they have a job ticket that will support them throughout their working life or until they save enough money to start a business, go to college, or whatever. To the job skills, add the valuable experience in business in general and the lessons in human nature. Business is a great school. You learn to take your *report cards* very seriously.

Mind your own business

If you aren't self-employed, or if you choose not to take your child into the business with you, it might be a good idea to help him start a business of his own. The advantage to doing this before he reaches adulthood is that he can do it with much less pressure. Because he can live at home where Daddy pays the bills, he doesn't have to make a living wage at his business. He won't have to put in the long hours that many self-employed people do. He also doesn't have to be afraid to experiment and speculate, because success or failure in the first year is not of critical importance. Because the profits from his work don't have to be spent on living expenses, he can use a greater part of it to reinvest in the business. There is no reason that a young man, starting a small business in his midteen years, couldn't be making plenty of money to support a family by age twenty.

There are several limitations on a young person doing this, but they can be overcome. Lack of a driver's license, shortage of capital, and the unwillingness of potential customers to do business with a minor may be among the drawbacks to this system. Some businesses would be impossible under such circumstances, but your child only needs one business. If he can't start out doing what he wants to do, let him start out doing something he doesn't want to do until such time as he has accumulated the maturity, capital, and experience to enter his chosen field. As his knowledge and assets grow, so does the scope of his opportunities.

What sort of a business can a teenager operate? There are quite a number in spite of the limitations. One summer of working for a paint contractor would be enough experience for a young man to start contracting on his own. I had far less experience than that when I started, and with the help of books and experienced counsel I managed to scrape out at least a meager living for a wife and children even the first year. A friend of mine buys wrecked cars, which he repairs, repaints, and sells at a considerable profit. That would be a good idea for a young mechanical type.

For the more academically oriented, modern computer technology offers quite a range of possible services to sell. Furniture making might be a good home industry. The list goes on.

One father offered this advice: "Son, there are only six words that express what you do in business—find a need and fill it." That's the idea. In fact one of the advantages of self-employment is that the perpetual responsibility to satisfy customers creates an alertness to the needs of others.

Climb the job ladder

With the modem philosophy of career development so oriented around school diplomas and automatic postgraduate job offers, this old-fashioned method has fallen into disrepute. But it's just as valuable as it ever was and many a young person has learned that the hard way after having found college unsuitable and dropped out.

Andrew Carnegie was a Scottish boy who came to America in 1844 at the age of thirteen. He had little schooling and never went to school after coming to this country. Shortly after arriving, he went to work in a cotton factory for $1.20 *per week*. At fifteen he took a job delivering telegrams and by seventeen had taught himself to send and decipher telegraph messages so well that he was able to land a job as a telegraph operator. Carnegie's next job was one of railroad clerk in the office of a division superintendent of the Pennsylvania Railroad. He worked his way up to dispatcher and while doing so used his small salary to make some investments that later paid off handsomely. When his chief was promoted to vice-president of the company, Carnegie replaced him as division manager. Later he entered the iron industry and in 1873 visited a steel plant that aroused his enthusiasm for the possibilities in the steel business. He built his own steel plant with the earnings of his job and investments. His business grew and in 1899 he merged his enterprises into the Carnegie Steel Company. That company became one of the greatest industrial enterprises in the country. When Andrew Carnegie retired, his fortune had reached half a billion dollars, making him one of the richest men in the world at the time. He devoted the rest of his life to giving that money away through a number of philanthropic projects such as the Carnegie Libraries, the Carnegie Institute of Technology, and a benefit fund for the employees of Carnegie Steel.

I don't suggest that Carnegie's success was typical of people who start their careers in entry-level jobs, but it illustrates the potential. Many a man who starts out low on the totem pole ends up near the top. And many a man who started out working for the other guy has accumulated the knowledge and capital by hard work and savings to start his own business later on. Maybe the reason more people don't do the same is that we are all so spoiled to luxury and credit buying that we've lost the patience to save. We must have our impressive cars and our high-tech stereo systems and so we throw away our future possibilities and end up with debts instead of investments.

A friend of mine started out as a high school dropout, flipping hamburgers at minimum wage. He worked his way up to management, then entered a partnership to buy his first restaurant. After a few years he bought his partner out and began to add restaurants to his chain. By the time he reached his mid-thirties he was a respected and successful business owner.

A lot of people start out in minimum-wage jobs, but not all of them end up financially successful. The main difference I can see is that those who succeed have the vision and drive to go higher and the self-discipline to work hard and manage their earnings wisely. They are also willing to take carefully calculated risks. Others, and even some skilled craftsmen among them, never look beyond doing what they have been doing for thirty years and take the raises and layoffs as they come. It's not the low beginning that determines the outcome, but the low or high motivation of the worker.

If your young person chooses the entry-level job route, there is no reason he can't have a fabulously successful career. But he needs to look farther down the road than the pluses and minuses of his first position. If he wants to be self-employed at some point, he should scout for a job in the field in which he wants to work. That way he can gain not only good work habits, job skills and capital, but also a general orientation to his chosen line of business. If he thinks he'd rather rise in rank within an established company than look toward the responsibility of business ownership, he will need to look for a company that is large enough to give him room to grow. After all, you can't climb very high on a ladder with only three rungs.

A Final Thought

Whether your child serves an apprenticeship, goes to trade school, enters the family business, starts a business of his own, works his way up the job ladder or lands in an executive position fresh out of grad school, it is his character that will determine God's blessing and your young person's success. The best preparation we can give our children is to concentrate not on what they have or what they know, but who they are. And that preparation begins early in life as they learn in their own homes the diligence, honesty, prudence, creativity, determination, and orderliness that are the foundation of success in any enterprise. If we teach them by example to be responsible and to always keep growing, we can give them a great leg up.

Chapter 12
About College

I F YOU'RE STANDING at a book table and have just picked up this book in the search for a volume to tell you everything you need to know to about getting your child a college education, I suggest you put it back down. I am totally unqualified to coach you on that subject. My own college career consisted of dropping out of three different majors in three different schools.

The first time I went to college I was eighteen years old, a fresh high school graduate and absolutely devoid of common sense and direction. After having played my way through high school earning no higher honor than that of being voted Wittiest Senior, I was no closer to finding my life's work than I had been when I graduated from eighth grade. I chose a boring little college in a boring little town, rented a boring little apartment and took a bunch of boring little subjects. My career goal at that time was to loaf through school, get a degree and take a job teaching speech and drama in a high school, coaching the school wrestling team on the side. I guess I had enjoyed playing my way through high school so much that I planned to do it for the rest of my life.

But a semester and a half was all the boredom I could take, so I joined the Air Force and in so doing signed up for four full years of boredom. But while in the Air Force, I met the true love of my life (ain't that romantic), got married, had our first child, and came to the conclusion that I wanted to spend my career in the ministry. This led me to move to Virginia when I was discharged and enroll in a Christian college with a major in youth ministry. But the financial and emotional demands of a young family were too much for me at that age and I decided that God had things to teach me that I wasn't learning in class. So I took a year off from school which turned into several.

I had concluded that I wasn't yet ready for the ministry and so I took a full-time job in law enforcement work. A couple of years later I went back to school at a community college, planning to get a degree in police science. But before I could complete the program I was offered an attractive job with a sheriffs department and eventually I let school go by the wayside. I ended up with about two years' college, all scrambled up between three unrelated majors and most of it useless to me.

My experience is not unusual except that I dropped out perhaps more times than most students. Still, many people go straight through four years of college, land a good job, and are very satisfied with their career development. So my opinion is that college is certainly a useful option, though it's not for everybody.

But I react against the widespread assumption that one must go to college to be successful in a career and to make the most of his abilities. I offer the lives of Benjamin Franklin, Thomas Edison, Andrew Carnegie, and legions of other unschooled geniuses as proof. But at the same time, be advised that I approach the subject as one who knows much more about the limitations of college than its advantages. I hope I have come to have an open mind on the subject, but because I feel that the population in general is prejudiced toward college as a necessity, I have a tendency to support the opposite view.

I have a friend who has a master's degree and additional graduate work in the computer field. He is absolutely sold on formal education because he has found his own schooling to be essential in pursuing his career in

255

About College Chapter 12

computer science. He and I have carried on friendly but extended arguments about the merits and limitations of college education more than once.

It finally came to me during one of these debates that the reason he was more in favor of college and I was more disposed toward the alternatives was a matter of goals. His interest was in the field of computers, which evidently is something to which the college environment lends itself quite well. My interest was in the ministry and the field of education, both of which I believe have been damaged by too much institutionalization. When I mentioned this he agreed with me, and at the same time I admitted that a college degree is sometimes necessary for landing a job even if the course work doesn't really prepare the man for doing the job. "That's right, Rick," my friend affirmed. "It's a key. It opens doors."

There is a perverse streak in me that rebels against the idea of a man spending four years of his life to obtain a piece of paper that he must have in order to get hired, then finding out that the things he has studied during those years don't equip him to do the job. That's not a rare occurrence, as was demonstrated to me once at a home-education convention where I was speaking on the father's role.

There were about a hundred men in my workshop and when I asked for a show of hands to indicate how many of them had college degrees, every hand went up with no more than one or two exceptions. I was surprised to learn that nearly everybody present had a degree except little old me, the workshop speaker. In fact, it was a little intimidating. Here I was, the three-time dropout, lecturing

Chapter 12 **About College**

a bunch of guys who had finished the course. For a minute I could almost feel my knuckles dragging the ground.

Then I asked my second question: *How many of you now have, or have ever had, a job which you couldn't have gotten without your degree, but which had very little to do with the material you studied to get that degree?* At least half of the hands went back up. I found that a little startling. I had heard men say before that they had been in such a position, but I hadn't expected such a high percentage. I don't claim that my workshop group was representative of the general population, but I think we should be concerned that such a ratio exists among my group of college-educated men.

Just to clear the air, let me say at this point that I am not saying you should not send your child to college. What I am saying is that you should give your child whatever form of education best prepares him for the life God has called him to lead. If that involves college, fine. But college is not the best preparation for every career. I discussed several alternatives in the previous chapter so I won't review those here, but let me say again that we live in a hyperschooled society and you may need to be careful that you give the other routes full consideration rather than going with the flow and mothballing your child in college for four years.

College=Education. Not.

Many times during the past several years I have asked myself how I should have gone about pursuing my education rather than fumbling around as I did. At the same time, of course, I've had to deal with the issue on behalf of my children. As I've worked through a lot of philosophical fodder some thoughts have occurred to me that have opened my eyes to things I never saw back in my own school days. Based on my experience, reading, reflection and discussion with others, I would advise a young person to do things quite differently.

To start with, I would not advise committing to a college major. If you attend college at all, use it as a cafeteria. Take what you want and leave the rest. How do you know what courses to take? First of all, take what sounds interesting. Drop courses that you don't find interesting or useful. Find people who know about your chosen career field and ask them what you can find in the college catalog that will actually help you. But don't limit yourself to courses that have to do with your job interest; there are more reasons to learn than just to earn money. Above all, discuss it with your parents and heed their counsel.

You need to be aware that if you approach college this way, the rules change. If you don't declare a major you will disqualify yourself from some scholarships and I think there are even some schools that won't enroll you at all. You will also run into some in the school hierarchy who will try to put pressure on you to declare, believing that a degree is a necessity. Listen to their reasoning but don't accept it as inspired. There are too many idiots with degrees.

School is not an education. We tend to ask each other about our educational histories in terms of years, but no two people gain the same amount of learning from a year's schooling. My buddy Butch, the lawyer's son, graduated the same night I graduated, and from the same school. So did over two hundred other people. But I had learned nowhere near as much as had Butch in high school. He had actually studied. As a matter of fact, I wouldn't really care to speculate on how I compared to the other two hundred graduates.

When we ask a person how much education he has had, we're not asking how much he knows. There's no way of accurately measuring that. What we're really asking is how long the other person spent in an institution of learning. So the next time someone asks you how much education you have, don't worry about trying to explain all that you know. Just tell him how long you were kept in an institution.

I would not advise going to college full time right after high school. Most young people don't seem to know enough about their life direction to make good use of their schooling, as evidenced by the high dropout rate. Stay home with your parents, take a useful job (or make one for yourself), learn some profitable skills, and experience the real world for a while. Make yourself useful at home. Your parents have supported you all your life; now try to make things easier for them. Help train your younger siblings, clean the house, mow the yard. Cultivate your hobbies and talents. One of them may be the key to your future career, and one or several of them may be useful in ministering for the LORD, such as with music for example. Spend time serving others, either by involvement in the programs of your local church or in some creative channel based in your home, such as writing to or visiting shut-ins, distributing Christian literature, or the like.

Active involvement in the business of living is the best context for effective learning. If all young people would stay at home with their parents while pursuing higher education, there would be far fewer instances of students tossing away their parents' values to experiment in drugs, immorality, or the philosophies of Godless instructors. Besides that, the time the student spends involved with the affairs of home, church, workplace, and community serve as a philosophical anchor. Those affairs of daily living are a constant reminder of what knowledge is really important and useful.

While you are learning by *doing*, be learning by *pursuing*. Read, read, read. I found out in college that I could pass many courses by doing no more than paying attention in class and reading the textbook. If the book is that large a hunk of the course, think how much you could learn about the same subject if you read three or four books on it. If you read a lot you will become a good reader and good readers can read with both speed and retention. I read an autobiography of a man who for a period of months read a book a day. An average reader could read a solid book per week and have lots of time for other activities as well. He would be reading around fifty books a year which, if they were well chosen, would be providing him with much more and better learning than most people ever get from a year of college.

One little-known benefit of reading rather than taking college courses is that it makes available more of the knowledge of the professor. That sounds ridiculous, but the fact is that many highly respected college professors spend much more time researching and writing than they do in the classroom. It is the research and writing work, not the classroom work, that brings the greatest income to both the professor and the school—the professor through career advancement, and the school through increased donations resulting from increased prestige. The upshot of this is that you can take a course with Professor Jones listed as the instructor and seldom see Professor Jones, his classes usually being taught by a teaching assistant who often is a graduate student. So if you want to get the full benefit of Professor Jones' knowledge, read his books rather than taking his classes.

Of course, it is possible to attend college and read voraciously at the same time. But most people don't. Why not? Because they use up so much of their time and energy reading and reporting on materials required for class that they don't want to even see another book, unless it's purely entertainment in content. I think we need to reconsider what four years of this conditioning does to a young person.

Einstein himself said that when he graduated from school it was over a year before he could stand to concentrate on scientific matters, so burned out was he from the school regimen.

I have a friend who taught in a university school of education and for some years was their chairman of graduate studies. I once asked him how many of his education majors ever went to the school library and checked out a book on the topic of education not for an assignment, but just because they were interested in it. He didn't think long before answering that three out of a hundred would be an optimistic guess.

I was shocked. That university is ten minutes from my home and I have been down there many times, checking out piles of education-related books on my community user card. It's hard for me to imagine that ed majors, most of whom live on campus, don't have families to care for and don't work full-time jobs, would waste the incredible resources in that library. It's been a gold mine for me. Yet waste it they do, and I have to believe that it is in large part because they are burned out on books and papers related to school requirements. It's really no wonder that they feel a need to spend their spare time doing anything other than reading.

It's worthwhile to ponder a bit too, on how the reading and other requirements of the school regimen affect the actual thinking and learning processes of students. When I used to read for an assignment, I found I was conditioned to think in a way that was different from and inferior to my usual way of thinking. When I read assigned material, my concentration was not on remembering the information for the sake of having it to use, but on remembering it for the sake of being evaluated on it. I was learning to think in terms of satisfying someone else, of predicting and answering questions imposed from without. They decided what was important to read, they formulated questions about it, and they applied sanctions designed to induce me to answer their questions in a certain way. If I jumped through their hoop, they gave me a dog biscuit.

This system habituated me to memorize data in such away that I could recall enough of it to pass a test, but forgot it soon thereafter. I don't know how to explain how I did it, but it was rather like swallowing information and then regurgitating it on a test paper. I was a mental

bulimic, ingesting information in quantity but disgorging it without it having been assimilated enough to nourish me.

When I read nowadays, nobody is evaluating me. I read because I enjoy it (though I don't read nearly as much as I would like to because of time constraints) and because I feel responsible to learn. I am bought with a price; I am not my own (1 CORINTHIANS 6:19–20). Therefore I feel obligated to learn as much as I can about the things that will make me most useful to God in the arena in which He has placed me.

Because I'm reading to meet real needs, I think differently and more effectively than when I used to read for school. I am more interested in what I read, which automatically makes a night-and-day difference in my comprehension and retention. I find myself asking myself questions: Is this true? Can I validate it by my own experience or previous knowledge? Is this important? How important is it? Why is it important? How much is the author's personal bias reflected in this? What basis does he have for his opinions? How can I use this information? I wonder what other authorities agree and disagree with this writer?

When reading for school assignments I asked different questions. What are they going to ask me about this? What methods of association or other tricks can I use to remember it? What points can I bring up in class discussion or essay questions to make me appear to know more than I do?

The skills learned to glean, digest, and retain useful information are totally different from the skills cultivated to satisfy an evaluator. Reading for need (or interest) inculcates the skills of gaining and keeping that which I have reason to believe is important. Reading for grades habituates the reader to think in terms of playing a game, manipulating a system in which knowledge is not the ultimate goal, but just one of several factors in gaining favor in the eyes of the evaluator. Instead of reading in search of facts to use in the real, live world, I read for clues to what the teacher will ask me about the reading. Instead of thinking about what will life require of me, I'm thinking: *what will the artificial economy of school require of me?* The system to which I am bound by symbolic carrots and sticks steals energy from learning and offers it as a sacrifice to paper gods.

It also taught me to be a test technician rather than a motivated learner. Instead of concentrating on learning all I could, I taught myself to beat the system. For instance, I learned that on essay tests, I was rewarded for volume. The more I wrote, the better my score. I learned that on multiple choice tests the process of elimination made it easier, as one of the four choices was always ridiculous and one other at least unlikely, leaving me with a fifty-fifty chance of guessing correctly between the remaining two. I found out that it pays to reflect the instructor's prejudices. If he seemed to feel that Hawthorne was a great writer, I would get a better grade on an essay if I praised Hawthorne above other authors (which also conditioned me to be a liar, because I detest Hawthorne). I also found that it paid to ask lots of questions and be vocal in class discussions. It makes the teacher think he's motivating you, which strokes his ego. In response, he will have a subconscious tendency to favor you.

When all is said and done, tests measure memory more than anything. The student who has a good memory may score much higher than the student who is a real learner—searching, pondering, exploring, comparing, wondering, experimenting. But it is not the memorizer, the intellectual bulimic who will succeed in the big, wide world outside the hallowed halls. It's the other guy, the one who has learned not how to anticipate and memorize test matter, but who can look at his environment, see a need, and go about formulating his own important questions and answers in finding a way to meet the need. I wish I had some good research data to tell me statistically how high test scorers perform in their careers compared to the rest of us. The only study I've read about thus far is quite an old one (1950's) and I believe that was in William Glasser's book, *Schools Without Failure.* Though it was done too long ago to be of any great credibility now, the study did show that men who had been high scorers on school tests, when tracked through twenty or thirty years of their careers, performed with significantly less success than their less scholastic peers.

The false economy in school would be obvious to persons less habituated to schooling than we. Look at the concept of the grade point average (GPA) for a clear example. Let's say for instance, that you're a college student with a pre-med major. You're going to go to medical school after college and become a doctor. This semester you have a course in chemistry and a course in Oriental architecture. Which course is more important to your life? Why, chemistry without question. Which course is more important to your GPA? Neither! They have an exactly equal effect. A low grade in Oriental architecture will hurt your GPA just as much as a low grade in chemistry, and in so doing hurt your chances of acceptance to med school just as much. Thus, the system requires you to put just as much effort into courses that have little value to you as any other, meaning automatically less effort into more important ones. The grading system is the enemy of your career priorities.

Real World, Real Learning

Thomas Edison once tried approximately ten thousand experiments with a storage battery and had still not found the key to the problem. When a friend expressed condolences at what he assumed was Mr. Edison's discouragement, he found that there was no discouragement. "Why, I haven't failed," the inventor replied. "I've just found ten thousand ways that won't work."

Minds such as Edison's, those that formulate questions, theories and experiments, are not produced by reading workbooks and writing down the answers to the quiz at the end of the chapter. Nor was the mind of the great Benjamin Franklin, or Bedford Forrest, the semi-literate but self-taught military genius of the civil war. Those men attained greatness in their fields by following their interests, seeing the practical needs around them and going about finding answers with organization, creativity and long hours of hard work.

The same results can be obtained by your children in the same way. College may be helpful to them, but you must not allow them to be caught in the old trap of chasing grades rather than knowledge. They must also resist the temptation to let college dominate their time so that they lose their moorings in the real world of work, family, ministry, and community. I'm open to some college attendance for my children, but I will not be the least bit disappointed if none of them ever darkens the door of a classroom. I want them to be lifelong learners, servers, producers, and leaders. As Newton D. Baker said,

> *The man who graduates today and stops learning*
> *tomorrow is uneducated the day after.*

... ...

Afterword

I N THE FIRST CHAPTER of this book I told you that we had four purposes in writing it. Those purposes were to encourage you, to give you some Biblical principles on which to operate, to supply some practical ideas for the job, and to give you an enjoyable time. If we've accomplished each of those, at least to some degree, then the work of writing, even for a bona fide computer idiot, has been well worthwhile.

But as we part company I want to reiterate my firm belief that you, the parent, don't need a lot of help from the Boyers or anybody else. Thousands of families have already proven that ordinary parents can produce extraordinary children simply by trusting in God and using their best judgment. Education does not depend upon buildings, resources, specialists and equipment, but on cultivating the inborn urge to know and to do and to become. The natural and most effective way for that to happen is in the environment of the family.

When all is said and done, education, as every other important enterprise of life, is a spiritual battle. God loves families and so Satan hates them. So when times come in which you feel that you're doing things to the best of your ability and yet the results aren't what you had hoped, go back to God. Claim the blood of Jesus in regard to every difficulty the enemy of your soul can present, then move ahead on the assumption that God is in control, that the principalities and powers are under His dominion, and that all will be well regardless of present appearances. As you pray, the Boyers are praying with you.

All that said, please accept my congratulations on your willingness to invest the time and effort to give your children the very best you have. I firmly believe that

~ **Afterword**

the mighty wave of which you are a part, is a turning back of the fathers' hearts to the children, which God promised in MALACHI 4:6 would cause the hearts of the children to turn to their fathers and the withholding of God's curse from our land. Others may think that America has sunk too far to be redeemed, but God's hand is not shortened. He has promised that if His people, who are called by His name, would humble themselves, pray, seek His face and turn from their wicked ways, He will hear, forgive, and heal their land. Listen to the hum of parents' voices at a gathering of home educators and you will hear within it the stirring of dry bones.

I look forward with eagerness to see what God will do with your children in His movement to make America once again a city on a hill.